CONTEMPORARY,

PSYCHOLOGY

Contemporary Psychology
Dept. of Psychology
University of Texas
Austin, Texas   78712

Conceptual Issues
in
Operant Psychology

Conceptual Issues in Operant Psychology

P. Harzem and T. R. Miles
Department of Psychology
University College of North Wales
Bangor

JOHN WILEY & SONS

Chichester · New York · Brisbane · Toronto

Library of Congress Cataloging in Publication Data:

Harzem, P
  Conceptual issues in Operant psychology.

  Includes index.
    1. Operant conditioning. 2. Psychology—Philosophy.
  I. Miles, Thomas Richard, joint author. II. Title.
  BF319.5.06H38   152.3'224   77–21280

ISBN 0 471 99603 3

Typeset by Preface Ltd., Salisbury, Wiltshire
Printed in Great Britain by Unwin Brothers Ltd.,
The Gresham Press, Old Woking, Surrey

In an age wherein we hear so much of thinking and reasoning, it may seem needless to observe how useful and necessary it is to think, in order to obtain just and accurate notions, to distinguish things that are different, to speak consistently, to know even our own meaning. And yet, for want of this, we see many, even in these days, run into perpetual blunders and paralogisms.

George Berkeley
Theory of Vision Vindicated, section 70.

Contents

Preface

This book combines ideas from two separate sources. The first of these is the total body of research which comes under the head of 'operant psychology' and which owes its origin primarily to B. F. Skinner. The second is the set of techniques which have been developed in philosophy in the last 50 years and which are associated in particular with the names of Ludwig Wittgenstein, J. L. Austin, and Gilbert Ryle. Our main task will be to make use of these techniques in modifying and advancing the programme of operant psychology.

Our title refers to 'conceptual' issues. We are in fact primarily concerned with the language–or, more strictly, with the concepts–which operant psychologists use in the course of their research. These include the concepts of *reinforcer*, *discriminative stimulus*, *response rate*, and many others; and psychologists who use these concepts differ in important ways in their approach from those who speak of *unconscious motives*, from those who claim to measure *IQ*s, from those who study *personal constructs*, and so on. To choose a particular set of concepts is in effect to decide to do psychology in a particular way. We shall be concerned with what has been called the 'logical behaviour' of concepts (cf. Chapter 2). Without a proper understanding of such behaviour there is danger that psychologists may mislead both themselves and their readers by giving inappropriate descriptions of what they are trying to achieve.

Those psychologists who have dismissed the contribution of the philosopher as irrelevant to their purposes may have had wrong expectations. In particular they may have accepted uncritically the assumption that the philosopher is a kind of 'armchair' psychologist who talks in a learned way about human nature (or even about animal nature) but does not base his claims on systematic experiment. Any 'help' which he might offer to psychologists would on this showing be of somewhat dubious value, since most of the characteristics associated with the methods of science–objectivity, systematic observation, quantification, etc.–would by definition be lacking. To carry conviction he would need to abandon unsubstantiated guesses and rely instead on the results of systematic experiment.

If the philosopher were trying to answer the same kinds of question as the psychologist this argument would be compelling. In the present book, however, we shall be giving him a different role. Indeed it will be unhelpful from our point of view to distinguish 'the' philosopher from 'the' psychologist at all, since anyone who attempts to deal with conceptual issues in psychology can for our purposes be said to be philosophizing. The important point, however, is not what the activity is called (the expression 'second-order psychology' would perhaps be equally good); our concern is to exhibit the need both for a critical examination of psychological concepts and for the drawing of a distinction between such examination and the reporting of research findings. To put the matter in a somewhat provocative way, what matters most in psychology is not the findings as such but what one *says* about them.

It is unfortunately true that some authors of psychology books, particularly when they state their programme in the early chapters, have failed to appreciate the amount of muddle which can arise from bad philosophizing. There are in fact certain techniques which need to be learned (and which we shall be describing in Chapters 2 and 3) by anyone who wishes to discuss conceptual issues with any proficiency. It is pointless to ask *whether* psychologists should philosophize (in our sense of the word), since discussion of conceptual issues is unavoidable; the important question is whether they do so explicitly and in full awareness of what is involved or whether they indulge unwittingly in second-rate philosophy of an amateur kind. In this connection we are in full agreement with Vesey (1974, p. 450), who writes: 'By all means let psychologists philoso-phise. But let them be aware that they are doing so.' Psychologists who belittle the contribution of philosophy should also bear in mind a warning given by Scriven (1956, p. 88), who says: 'Those who cry "No politics" often thereby support bad politics, and those in whose prefaces philosophy is abjured often proceed to expound bad philosophy'.

One of our guiding principles has been the insistence that where there is controversy in psychology one should bring rational methods to bear in attempting to resolve it. Some disagreements can be settled by further research or by a reconsideration of the available evidence. Sometimes, however, there are more basic disagreements which reflect differing views on the ways in which data should be classified and on the questions which can helpfully be asked about such data; and here one usually finds the adoption by the two parties of differing sets of concepts. In either case it is important to be clear what the disagreement is about; otherwise there will merely be misunderstanding and failure of com-munication—evils which unfortunately have bedevilled operant psychology from its outset. We are opposed in particular to what may be called 'point scoring' in academic debate. All too often psychology students are encouraged to think in 'polarized' terms—Chomsky versus Skinner, mentalism versus behaviourism, psychotherapy versus behaviour therapy, nature versus nurture, dualism versus materialism, etc. They are thus encouraged to believe that they should take sides and defend one member of the pair by disposing of the other in a few brief sentences. It does not seem to have occurred to them that thinkers of stature seldom make elementary blunders (which, anyway, would not normally be worth serious discussion); and it is our experience that 'ideological' debate of this kind is unprofitable. In a sense, no doubt, our views can be described as 'pro' operant psychology and 'pro' the philosophical techniques of Wittgenstein,

Austin and Ryle (else why write a book of this kind?), but it is not our intention to 'win' any kind of argument or 'prove' that Skinner or Ryle or anyone else was right, or even that they were wrong. Indeed, one advantage of the philosophical techniques which we shall be using is that, if suitably applied, they take the heat out of a number of controversies. As will be made clear in Chapter 2, many conceptual questions can be fully answered if one points out both the reasons for saying 'yes' and the reasons for saying 'no'.

Chapter 1 will be an attempt to set operant psychology in its historical context, while Chapters 2 and 3 will introduce the reader to the relevant philosophical techniques. In Chapter 4 we examine some of the different attempts to characterize the subject matter of psychology and try to show that these can helpfully be regarded as commendations of alternative conceptual schemes. Chapters 5 to 8 contain discussion of conceptual issues which relate to operant psychology as a whole; in Chapter 9 we consider those conceptual issues which relate in particular to clinical psychology, while Chapters 10 and 11 are concerned with the implications of the operant approach for political and social issues. Finally, in Chapter 12, we discuss possible future developments with special reference to operant research with human subjects.

Earlier versions of Chapters 6, 7, 8, and 10 were presented as papers at meetings of the British Psychological Society and the Experimental Analysis of Behaviour Group, but all four chapters have been considerably modified since that time.

In conclusion, we should like to express out thanks to the many people whose ideas have contributed to the writing of this book, and particularly to our colleagues in the Department of Psychology at University College, Bangor, and to students over a decade. A special acknowledgement is due to Dr C. F. Lowe and Mr M. Bagshaw for their contributions to Chapter 12. We should also like to convey our gratitude to Professors A. R. White and A. G. N. Flew, both of whom were kind enough to read an earlier draft of the book; and although neither is responsible for the mistakes which remain, we have made free use of the many suggestions which they generously offered. Finally we should like to thank Mrs Llio Ellis-Williams for her skill and patience in converting illegible manuscript into typescript.

P.H.
T.R.M.
Bangor, 1977

Chapter 1

Historical Introduction

When Galileo caused balls, the weights of which he had himself previously determined, to roll down an inclined plane; when Torricelli made the air carry a weight which he had calculated beforehand to be equal to that of a definite column of water . . . a light broke upon all students of nature . . . Accidental observations, made in obedience to no previously thought-out plan, can never be made to yield a necessary law, which alone reason is concerned to discover. Reason . . . must approach nature . . . not . . . in the character of a pupil who listens to everything that the teacher chooses to say but of an appointed judge who compels the witnesses to answer questions which he has himself formulated.

So wrote Kant at the end of the eighteenth century (*Critique of Pure Reason*, Preface to second edition). The basic notion of 'putting questions to nature' is of course fundamental in what is now called 'scientific method'; and the successes which have come about in the study of chemical, physical (including electrical) and, more recently, biological phenomena are undisputed. At first glance, therefore, it is perhaps puzzling that the application of scientific method to the study of man and his affairs should have given rise to such a large amount of controversy.

In this book we shall try to show that apparently conflicting ideas about the scientific study of man can be resolved neither by belittling the achievements of science nor by 'reducing' man to something less than human, but by careful examination of certain crucial conceptual issues. It is often assumed that if one adopts an operant approach one is on the side of those who wish in some way to 'reduce' man. In our view such an assumption is unjustified; and in what follows we shall offer a version of operant psychology which insists on full scientific rigour but which cannot be open to the charge of being inhumane.

Even before Kant's time many of the difficulties which arise in treating man scientifically had been clearly appreciated. This becomes particularly apparent if one studies the writings of Descartes. Although philosophy textbooks normally present him as someone primarily concerned with deductive reasoning about the self and God and about the trustworthiness or otherwise of our senses, this picture is perhaps somewhat one-sided. One of the important influences on his thinking, for example, was Harvey's work on the circulation of the blood, and in

Part V of the *Discourse on Method* he suggests that readers may like to arrange to be present at the dissection of the heart 'of some large animal possessed of lungs', since this will lead to a better understanding of what he has to say. There is no clear distinction in his writings between 'philosophy' and 'science'; and it is important to recognize that his contributions to what we now call 'philosophy' can best be understood if we consider them in the light of the science of his day.

In particular, once it is appreciated that the blood flows in accordance with mechanical principles, it becomes an easy step to suppose that the same principles govern the workings of the body in general. Here is an interesting passage from the *Tract on Man*:

> You may have seen in grottoes and fountains in the royal gardens, that the force alone with which the water moves, in passing from the spring, is enough to move various machines, and even to make them play on instruments, or utter words, according to the different arrangement of the pipes which conduct it. And, indeed, the nerves of the machine that I am describing to you may very well be compared to the pipes of the machinery of these fountains, its muscles and its tendons to various other engines and devices which serve to move them, its animal spirits to the water which sets them in motion, of which the heart is the spring, and the cavities of the brain the outlets. Moreover, respiration and other such functions as are natural and usual to it, and which depend on the course of the spirits, are like the movements of a clock or a mill, which the regular flow of the water can keep up. External objects, which, by their presence alone, act upon the organs of its senses, and which by this means determine it to move in many different ways according as the particles of its brain are arranged, are like visitors who, entering some of the grottoes of these fountains, bring about themselves, without intending it, the movements which occur in their presence; for they cannot enter without stepping on certain tiles of the pavement, so arranged that, for example, if they approach a Diana taking a bath, they make her hide in the reeds; and if they pass on in pursuit of her, they cause a Neptune to appear before them, who menaces them with his trident; or if they turn in some other direction, they will make a marine monster come out, who will squirt water into their faces, or something similar will happen, according to the fancy of the engineers who construct them. And finally, when the *reasonable soul* shall be in this machine, it will have its principal seat in the brain, and it will be there like the fountain maker, who must be at the openings where all the pipes of these machines discharge themselves, if he wishes to start, to stop, or to change in any way their movements.

The reference to the fountain maker is, of course, crucial. Despite later criticisms, it was perfectly reasonable for Descartes to claim that human agents operated in some way independently of mechanical laws. In a letter to Henry More he writes:

Two different principles of our movements are to be distinguished — the one entirely mechanical and corporeal, which depends solely on the force of the animal spirits, and the configurations of the bodily parts, and which may be called corporeal soul, and the other incorporeal, that is to say, mind or soul, which you may define as a substance which thinks.

This idea of humans as independently operating causal agencies finds expression in a well-known passage (*Discourse on Method*, Part IV):

I thence concluded that I was a substance [i.e. a causal agency] whose whole essence or nature consists only in thinking, and which, that it may exist, has need of no place, nor is dependent on any material thing; so that 'I', that is to say, the mind by which I am what I am, is wholly distinct from the body, and is even more easily known than the latter.

We know of no serious thinker who has denied that there are important differences between humans and animals and between both of them and inanimate objects. What is controversial is not the existence of these differences but the question of how they can most appropriately be characterized. As we shall see later (Chapter 4), it is on this score that the Cartesian conceptual scheme is to some extent misleading.

If one makes the assumption, however, as most thinkers of the nineteenth century appear to have done, that 'mind' and 'matter' are two different kinds of entity or substance, then it is of course natural to ask whether there is any kind of 'concomitant variation' between the behaviour of the one and the behaviour of the other. Research aimed at answering this question was in fact described by Fechner as 'psycho-physics', since it involved (or appeared to involve) a study of the relationship between the entities existing in the mind (or 'psyche') and the entities existing in the 'physical' or 'material' world; and even if most psychologists nowadays would wish to describe the results of such research without using (or at least without taking seriously) the concepts of Cartesian dualism it by no means follows that the discoveries themselves were of no value. It was also widely assumed that since psychology is the study of mind its appropriate method ought to be that of 'looking into' the mind or introspecting; and this particular legacy of Cartesianism was no doubt in part responsible for the somewhat restricted set of topics which were chosen for study at the time. (See, for instance, the account by Humphrey (1951) of the investigations into thinking carried out by members of the Wurzburg school.)

It is worth noting that the methodological inadequacies which existed at this time were not due simply to lack of sophisticated equipment. Technological advances in the twentieth century have made it possible for psychologists to use highly elaborate devices for presenting stimuli and recording and quantifying responses—tachistoscopes of all degrees of complexity, timers, tape-recorders, on-line computers, and many other aids to research—but it is possible that their importance has been exaggerated. Absence of suitable equipment may result in measurements which are too inaccurate to be of use; and if data cannot be collected by automated means experimenters may sometimes have to rule out certain types of enquiry because of the labour involved in computation. As a matter of logic, however, such limitations cannot prevent the right questions from being asked. In particular the Skinner-box, which we shall be discussing in a moment, can be regarded as a triumph of *method* rather than of technology; and although in present-day operant research technological advances are being exploited in all kinds of ways, the provision of the basic hardware, at least in a primitive form, would have presented few difficulties even in a less technologically-minded age. A more important defect was the absence of any kind of agreement as to what sorts of questions were appropriate.

This did not, of course, mean that psychology could make no progress. The theory of evolution directed the attention of the biological sciences to the phenomenon of adaptation, and the result was a shifting of emphasis (particularly in functionalist psychology) to the question of how behaviour adapts to the environment. Although at first the process was taken to be that of natural selection, occurring over a large time scale, it was later recognized that the behaviour of an individual can adjust to the conditions and contingencies existing in a given environment. The idea that such adjustment could be usefully studied in its own right was destined to become central in operant psychology. Moreover, from the turn of the century onwards new and exciting discoveries were being made and fresh techniques of research were being developed. Among these were Thorndike's experiments on learning in animals, Pavlov's discovery of conditioning, and the research of Wertheimer, Köhler, Koffka, and Duncker into perception and problem solving. Psychology was now acquiring a content, and for many psychologists it no doubt seemed more important to try to explain and relate together the new findings and conduct further research rather than to discuss the seemingly more sterile questions of what psychology is and how it should proceed.

As a point of logic the next requirement was that the experimental findings should be incorporated in some more comprehensive view; and it was here that Skinner's insights played a particularly important part. His contributions to psychology can conveniently be classified under four heads, viz. (a) his insistence on the need to study the effect on an organism of the consequences of its behaviour, (b) the extension of this basic idea to the study of social situations, (c) his technical and methodological inventions, and (d) the new facts which he discovered.

(a) On Skinner's view the relationship between behaviour and its consequences is crucial, since some consequences 'reinforce' that behaviour, i.e. make it more probable in the future. Such consequences might be, for instance, a smile returned, an indication in some form or other that one has correctly solved a problem, a monetary reward, a pellet of food, or a whole range of other things. There is, however, a second, equally important relationship which modifies and 'controls' (in a sense to be discussed in Chapter 10) the occurrence of the behaviour that is reinforced. As everyone knows, an individual whose smile is reciprocated by someone he likes does not, from then on, go around with a bland smile on his face regardless of whether or not there is anyone near him. Similarly a typist who is paid for typing does not go through typing motions when she is at home and there is no typewriter at hand. Thus the presence of contextual cues, or 'discriminative stimuli', is necessary for the occurrence of a previously reinforced response. All cues that are reliably present at the time of reinforcement are likely to become discriminative stimuli with respect to the behaviour that is reinforced; that is to say, this behaviour occurs on future occasions only if the appropriate discriminative stimuli are present. The relationship between discriminative stimuli, behaviour, and reinforcement is named 'the three-term contingency'. Skinner's thesis is that the three-term contingency should be regarded as the fundamental unit in analysing and describing the behaviour of an individual, including his verbal behaviour.

(b) Skinner's views concerning the existing state of society and the ways of changing it are direct extensions of this thesis. Briefly, the conditions prevailing in a society at any one time are considered to be the consequences of the forms of behaviour that are reinforced in that society. What is required if a particular society is to be changed in directions approved by its members is that the existing contingencies of reinforcement should be adjusted, or, in other words, that steps should be taken to ensure that the desired behaviour is reinforced and that the undesired behaviour is not. Given that a technology is developed which allows for such adjustments in the availability of reinforcement, it will then be possible, according to Skinner, to construct a Utopia, that is, a society in which everyone leads a full and satisfying life.

(c) The invention of the Skinner-box marked an important turning-point in research techniques. As a result it became possible to investigate behaviour in an entirely new way. There are many instances in the history of science where the apparatus used has influenced the way in which researchers have conceived the phenomena in which they are interested, and this is true not least in psychology. For example, learning theorists who used mazes in their experiments have described the phenomena which they observed in terms of drives towards a *goal* and tendency to *approach* or *avoid*. In the same way the Skinner-box enables psychologists to view behaviour not as a series of discrete trials but as a continuous stream of repeated occurrences of an easily identifiable and recordable response and to observe any changes which occurred in that stream. To study behaviour in this way, without at the same time sacrificing experimental rigour, was new not only for animal experimenters but for psychology in general.

Although the Skinner-box in this respect represented an important departure from the established methods of research, it can also be seen as a further step in a line of continuous development in research methods and apparatus. The stages of this development are represented in Figure 1. The early mazes were too complicated to permit any clear analysis of the variables affecting the subjects' behaviour. Consequently a simpler maze was constructed, consisting of only

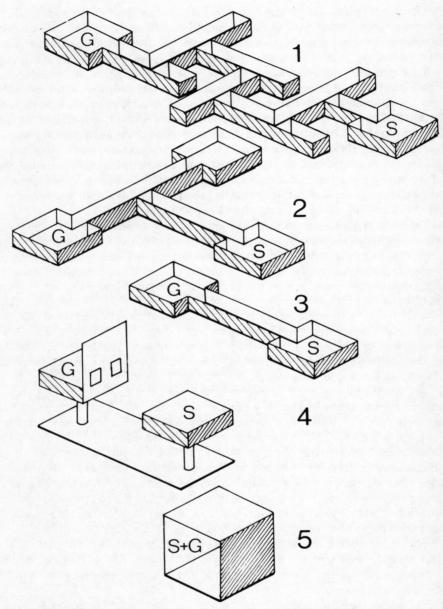

Figure 1 Schematic representation of the logical stages by which the complex mazes of early research evolved into the Skinner-box. Historically, of course, the different stages were overlapping rather than temporally distinct. The letters S and G stand for 'starting area' and 'goal' respectively. (Diagram drawn by M. Bagshaw)

one choice-point, namely a T-maze or a Y-maze. This also turned out to be too complicated, however, as it became apparent that an unwieldy number of variables could have been operating to determine the choice made. The next step was to remove the choice-point, leaving simply the straight runway between start-box and goal-box. Even in this apparatus, however, the required response, that is, traversing the length of the runway, was found to be difficult to observe and analyse. When Lashley removed the runway, the result was his well-known jumping-stand; and while the runway might be considered as a T-maze without the choice-point, the jumping-stand was in effect the choice-point without the runway, since the response of jumping incorporated within it the subject's choice. If one follows this line of development, the Skinner-box may be considered as consisting simply of the goal-box, or perhaps as being the result of a merger between the start-box and the goal-box. Here the subjects remained in what was physically the same space, and the experimenter studied how they adjusted to the conditions prevailing in that space. A development of prime importance was the provision of the lever, which made it possible to specify, in a precisely measurable and recordable way, the particular behaviour that was being investigated. If the subject was placed in a Skinner-box a record could be kept of the uninterrupted development of behaviour patterns in relation to their environmental context. There was also the further advantage that behaviour could be studied without the intervention of the experimenter. His role was simply to determine the conditions which were to prevail in the box and observe how the subject's behaviour came to terms with these conditions.

It is sometimes asserted, by way of criticism, that the Skinner-box creates an 'artificial' situation and that one cannot therefore use it to study what is likely to happen in 'real-life' situations. Ironically enough, precisely the opposite is the case: the use of a Skinner-box makes possible the experimental replication of those particular conditions of ordinary life which one has chosen for study.

It was standard practice in many early experiments to manipulate only one independent variable and to observe only one dependent variable. Thus in Skinner's initial research, which was concerned with relatively simple phenomena, the Skinner-box contained only one lever and the conditions in the box were held constant. It is not a logical requirement, however, that the events introduced by the experimenter into the box should be simple. They may be complicated as much as it is appropriate in the context of a given experimental problem. Sometimes, for instance, the complexity of the situation prevents the isolation of a single variable, or at times there may be a deliberate choice to study the interaction of two or more variables. The experiments may be concerned with questions such as how stable and persistent is any pattern of behaviour that develops under the particular experimental conditions, what are the effects of introducing a new condition into the situation, what are the effects of altering an existing condition, and so on. It will be noted that such a situation is like those in which an organism naturally exists. From birth it adjusts in various ways to the contingencies existing in its environment, some of these adjustments being stable and some not; and it behaves differently as the environment changes. In some circumstances organisms fail to adjust to new conditions or do so only slowly. If an experimenter decides to study these phenomena, he can best do so in an experimental situation where environment and behaviour are allowed to interact but which is at the same time sufficiently simple to facilitate the recording and study of their interaction. The Skinner-box is a device for conducting a wide range of investigations of this kind.

In principle, of course, the situation existing in a Skinner-box may be infinitely complicated. As the complexity is increased, the Skinner-box would approximate to the real world; and, conversely, if the real world were simplified in such a way that the fundamental relationships between an organism and its environment were retained, ultimately the result would be the situation that exists in a Skinner-box.

Another important innovation made by Skinner was that of measuring the response rate. This was a natural development arising from the use of the Skinner-box. Given that the repeated occurrences of a response are being studied, it is clearly appropriate to investigate the rate at which this happens. As a result psychologists were enabled to observe and record the changes in behaviour which took place during the course of an experiment and to relate these changes to other events such as the delivery of reinforcers. They were also enabled to develop the steady-state methodology, which involved first, the establishment of a steady response rate and, second, observation of the changes which occurred in consequence of experimental manipulations.

(d) The use of response rate as a measure enabled Skinner to describe the patterns of behaviour that are typically observed under the various 'schedules of reinforcement'. These studies constitute Skinner's important contribution to fact-finding in psychology (see especially Skinner, 1938). There appears to be some misunderstanding, however, with regard to the relevance of schedules of reinforcement in investigating the natural behaviour of organisms. Although it is likely that some of the basic schedules operate in some real-life situations, this is not to say that all natural relationships involving reinforcement conform to the simple arrangements involved in the basic schedules. It is, of course, possible to devise highly complex schedules for use in laboratory research, and conversely it is reasonable to assume that conditions that can be described in terms of complex schedules operate outside the laboratory. The investigations which are conducted with schedules of reinforcement are directed at discovering the principles that are common to the schedules, with the assumption that these principles would be also operating under real-life conditions. Research has already gone a long way along these lines, as is shown by the ever-increasing volume of literature on the subject; and although existing views on how to interpret and follow up these discoveries may come to be revised, the discoveries themselves are clearly of lasting value.

Since our purpose in this book is to discuss conceptual issues and not to review the research literature, we shall not be pursuing this matter further. In any evaluation of Skinner's work, however, it is important to bear in mind not only his emphasis on the three-term contingency and its applicability to the study of society (to both of which themes we shall be returning) but also his contribution to research methods and the interesting new facts which he discovered.

Chapter 2

On the Difference between Empirical and Conceptual Issues

If psychologists are to discuss conceptual issues with the necessary competence there are certain philosophical techniques with which they need to be familiar. In the next two chapters we shall try to indicate what these techniques are and the kinds of thing which they can achieve.

We claim no originality for any philosophical ideas which these chapters contain. Indeed, as far as philosophy is concerned, the points which we shall be making are commonplace; and while it may be true that philosophers sometimes disagree among themselves as to how and when particular arguments should be used (for example, the argument that such-and-such is 'not what we say in ordinary language'), anyone trained in this area of philosophy at least knows what techniques are available. Our purpose, therefore, is not to offer any distinctive contribution to philosophy but simply to set out the requisite background knowledge for the benefit of readers who are unfamiliar with the relevant literature. Among useful expository books may be mentioned in particular those of White (1967), Warnock (1969), Flew (1971), and Bontempo and Odell (1975). In addition many of the discussions to be found in Wisdom (1953) make fascinating reading.

As we shall see later, disagreement on philosophical issues (in our sense) is not impossible, but careful reflection is needed in that case as to what the disagreement is about; and there are in fact many philosophical insights which when stated are obvious. We are not, therefore, setting ourselves up as members of any particular philosophical 'school' or as defenders of any particular philosophical 'thesis'.

Some may say that the kind of philosophy which we are doing is 'empiricist' in character. This description, however, seems to us unsatisfactory. An 'empiricist', as we understand the term, is one who attaches some special kind of importance or primacy to what philosophers have called 'empirical statements' (see below) as opposed to statements of other kinds; and it is hard to see what sort of importance or primacy is intended or how such a claim could be justified. It will in fact be a central thesis of this book that language can be used for many different purposes, and we know of no good arguments for saying that empirical statements (however defined) deserve some sort of privileged status.

It may also be said that we are advocating a special type of philosophy often known as 'linguistic' philosophy. Here, too, we question the value of the label. It is true that some philosophers in recent decades, in their discussion of philosophical problems, have made a self-conscious attempt to study certain aspects of the functioning of language. The appropriateness of the term 'linguistic', however, is itself a philosophical question. It is not easy to find indisputable grounds for distinguishing 'linguistic' philosophy from other kinds of philosophy; and indeed, as Price (1945) has aptly pointed out, a traditional philosopher who believes himself to be discussing 'the nature of self' is not necessarily doing anything very different from those more recent philosophers who might claim that they were carrying out a linguistic analysis of sentences containing the word 'I'. In any case, whether the words 'linguistic philosophy' are helpful or not, it needs to be made clear that those who make use of the techniques described in the next two chapters are not thereby committed to any particular set of philosophical views. Indeed to say 'If you are a linguistic philosopher you must believe so and so' is extremely naive whatever the 'so and so' may be. It is true that implicitly we are making the claim that the techniques in question can be exploited to good purpose, or at any rate that it is justifiable to consider what can be done with them; but we do not do so in any spirit of philosophical dogmatism, nor are we committed to the view that exploitation of these techniques is the only right way to do philosophy.

We shall begin by calling attention to the need (emphasized in the quotation from Berkeley at the beginning of our book) for distinguishing things that are different. Not only is chalk different from cheese, and a tiger from a lion, but of special interest for present purposes is the differences between different *types of statement*. (It is of course true that words can be used for many purposes other than 'stating' something, e.g. 'Go away!', 'I agree', 'Alas!', etc.; but for present purposes this point need not concern us.) Thus the statements 'There is some cheese in the larder' and 'There are hundreds of lions in the game reserve' are like each other in respects in which both are unlike '50 + 50 = 100'. Many philosophers have attempted to classify statements into types. Thus Plato (*Republic*, vii, 529) emphasizes that the truths of mathematics are different from the discoveries which result from common-sense observation, while Aristotle (*Nichomachean Ethics*, I, iii, 4) says: 'It is the mark of a well-trained person to require, in each kind of inquiry, just so much exactness as the subject admits of: it is equally absurd to accept plausible argument from a mathematician and to demand logical proof from an orator.' Many centuries later Hume pointed out that 'experimental reasoning concerning matter of fact and existence' was different from 'abstract reasoning concerning quantity and number' and that both alike were different from the speculative metaphysics of the schoolmen (*An Enquiry Concerning Human Understanding*, xii, 3); and soon afterwards Kant, in the *Critique of Pure Reason*, showed how statements about God, freedom, and immortality were different from the statements of the physicist, e.g. 'Bodies fall when their supports are taken away', and different again from statements about the nature of space and time, e.g. 'Two straight lines cannot enclose a space'.

It is widely agreed nowadays that statements, along with biological specimens, illnesses, personality traits, types of weather, and much else, do not all fit tidily into particular classificatory schemes. There seems rather to be a complex web of similarities and differences. Statements—like things and people—can be like one another in some respects and not in others; and because of the diversity of use to which language can be put, it is perhaps wise to bear in mind the words of J. L. Austin (1962, p. 3) who suggests that philosophers should 'abandon the . . . worship of tidy-looking dichotomies'. If anyone doubts the value of this warning, let him attempt to classify under a small number of heads the following utterances: 'There's Helvellyn', 'There's the door!', 'Boys will be boys', 'Arsenic is poisonous', 'Jealousy is cruel as the grave', and 'All animals are equal but some animals are more equal than others'.

This does not mean, however, that no classifications are possible at all; and our next task is to attempt to characterize the various differences which philosophers have had in mind when they have distinguished empirical statements from conceptual ones. It is important, of course, not to ascribe to this distinction a greater importance than it deserves, but we hope that the discussions which occur later in the book will do something to establish its utility.

To illustrate the distinction let us consider the following statements: (1a) 'Smith is intelligent', (1b) 'To be able to remember digits correctly is not necessarily a sign of intelligence'; (2a) 'Smith is poorly motivated', (2b) 'Motives are not causes'; (3a) 'These tomatoes are red', (3b) 'Tomatoes are vegetables'; (4a) 'Memory declines in old age', (4b) 'There is no such entity as "*the* memory"'; (5a) 'Public opinion has veered round in support of the Prime Minister', (5b) 'There is no such entity as "public opinion"'.

Now there are, of course, many respects in which the (a)-statements differ from each other. Thus (1a) and (2a) are statements about particular people, whereas (4a) is a statement about memory in general; moreover (3a) can be checked by a single observation, whereas (1a), (2a), and (5a) all require a series of observations. Similarly the (b)-statements differ from each other in a variety of ways. In the discussion which follows, however, we shall be concerned not with these differences but with the ways in which the (a)-statements are like each other and are different from the (b)-statements.

For our purposes the most important point about the (a)-statements is that they all admit of being verified or falsified as a result of observation by the senses. To find out if Smith is intelligent or poorly motivated one observes him; similarly, to find out if certain tomatoes are correctly described as 'red' one observes them; to find out what happens to memory in old age one observes elderly people, and to find out if public opinion has veered round in support of the Prime Minister one observes a whole range of popular reactions when the Prime Minister's policy is discussed. Such statements are called 'empirical' because they are based on observation—on what we experience, *empeiria* being the Greek word for 'experience'.

A further important point about the (a)-statements is that they admit of what is called 'operational definition'. In other words their truth or falsity can be determined definitively as the result of a specifiable set of procedures or 'operations'. For example, to find out if Smith is intelligent one might go through the operations of giving him a specified intelligence test, and if he responds in certain ways then, provided the operational definition is agreed, it follows as a matter of logic that he is intelligent, since to be intelligent just *is* to respond in those specified ways.

We may note in passing that in ordinary language the operations implicit in words or expressions such as 'intelligent', 'poorly motivated', etc., are not specified to the last detail. To adapt a term used by Waismann (1945), ordinary language, unlike most technical languages used in science, is 'open-textured'. In this particular case, for example, there are all kinds of different things that Smith might do which would entitle one to say that he was intelligent or poorly motivated, and similarly with many other adjectives of ordinary speech, e.g. 'forgetful', 'cheerful', 'honest', etc. This lack of specificity is for many purposes an advantage: one can indicate a range of things which Smith is liable to do or has a propensity to do without being tied down to particular examples. There must, of course, be *something* about the situation which gives grounds for the use of such adjectives, since otherwise one would not be using them meaningfully; but that 'something' can be different on different occasions. In contrast there may be contexts, particularly those in which a scientific investigator carries out experiments which he wishes to be repeatable, where the operations need to be formulated in detail and with full precision. The importance of defining terms operationally may well vary from one context to another.

The (b)-statements, in contrast, do not necessarily predict that a specifiable occurrence will or will not take place, but they are concerned rather with the question, 'What *counts as* such and such? Thus in the case of (1b) there may be no dispute over the fact that Smith is able to remember digits correctly: the issue is whether ability to remember digits correctly counts as 'being intelligent'. Similarly in the case of (2b) there may be no dispute as to whether Smith was or was not poorly motivated; the issue here is whether, or in what sense, actions carried out from a certain motive, e.g. jealousy, can count as being 'caused' by that motive. Similarly it is being stipulated in (3b) that tomatoes should count as—or be classified as—vegetables, while in (4b) and (5b) the claim is that if certain happenings take place these on their own (without reference to any kind of enduring 'entity') should count as instances of memory or of a change in public opinion.

The (b)-statements have been characterized as 'conceptual' because in an important sense they are concerned with what philosophers call 'concepts'. Our particular examples dealt in fact with the concepts of *intelligence, motivation, vegetable, memory,* and *public opinion.* This does not mean, as is sometimes mistakenly supposed, that the issues simply relate to the correct or incorrect use of certain English words. This can be shown by pointing out that the same issues would arise in the case of words of equivalent meaning in any language at all; it makes sense to speak of English *words* but it is difficult to see what sense could be attached to speaking of 'English concepts'. Still less are conceptual discussions concerned with choice of words on aesthetic or stylistic grounds. They are concerned rather with what has been called the 'logical behaviour' of concepts, that is, with what is entailed (in the logicians' sense), or ought to be entailed, by their use. Thus one is making a conceptual point if one asserts that 'Smith is an uncle' entails 'Smith is male', since one is indicating what is entailed by the concept *being an uncle*. What has traditionally been called 'logic' can helpfully be regarded as the study of the logical behaviour of a restricted group of concepts, of which the most important are *if, all, some,* and *not.*

There is a complication here, however, in that the truths of logic are normally said by philosophers to be *necessary* truths, in contrast with the *contingent* truths afforded by empirical statements. A necessary truth, on this showing, is one whose opposite involves a self-contradiction; thus it would be self-contradictory to assert that Smith was an uncle if at the same time one denied that he was male. It does not follow, however, that we have now entered an area where the truth has been established beyond any possibility of doubt, since it is hard to see how the notions of 'doubt' and 'certainty' are applicable in a context of this sort. Indeed, if a person professed to dispute or doubt whether 'X is an uncle' entails 'X is male' one would simply conclude that he had misunderstood the meaning of one of the key terms, viz. 'uncle', 'entails', or 'male'. Moreover, while there may admittedly be situations in which a statement about the logical behaviour of a concept has only to be made to be accepted as obvious, there may also be situations (as we shall see more fully later in the chapter) where such statements are mistaken. It is therefore misleading to say that all conceptual statements involve necessary truths, even though some of them are not open to serious dispute.

Conceptual issues are important, we suggest, precisely in so far as correct classification is important. Not only do conceptual errors result in unnecessary muddle, but correct conceptual formulations can lead to all kinds of important insights. For example, once it is appreciated that there are many different happenings which can lead us to say that a person is intelligent, there is no longer any temptation to look for the 'true nature' or 'real meaning' of intelligence or to lament that we have not so far discovered it. More important, many major scientific advances have arisen as the result of proposals for reclassification. Sometimes this involves the coining of new technical terms and sometimes the use of existing words in a new way. Thus H_2O, *impedance*, and *neutron* are examples of the former, while the Copernican revolution in astronomy, which involves the claim that the earth, no less than Venus and Mars, should be classified as *a planet*, is an example of the latter. Similarly Darwin's great insight can be viewed as an example of conceptual innovation: he is saying that what happens in nature should count as a case of *selection*. In addition, though his view has not received universal acceptance, Freud could be interpreted as stipulating that when a child sucks at the breast this should be classified as a case of *sexual* activity.

There is, of course, an important difference between asserting that X *is* a case of Y and stipulating, or proposing, that X *should be regarded* as a case of Y. The person who asserts that a tomato is a vegetable would in most contexts be assumed simply to be indicating what is already implicit in the concept of a vegetable; in contrast, since an infant's sucking at the breast is not by definition a case of sexual activity, one is here confronted with a proposal that the concept of *sexuality* be *extended so as to include* infantile sucking at the breast. Within conceptual statements, therefore, it is helpful to distinguish two kinds, viz. (i) those which report on the logical behaviour of concepts, and (ii) those which commend proposals for conceptual change. The former may be said to involve *conceptual analysis*, the latter *conceptual revision*. Since the boundaries at which a concept ceases to be applicable are not always clearly defined, there may, of course, be situations where one is unsure if the speaker is reporting on existing boundaries or stipulating where a boundary should be drawn. For example, if someone says, 'To be able to repeat digits correctly is not necessarily a sign of intelligence', one is unsure whether this should be counted as part of an attempt to analyse the existing concept of *intelligence* or as a proposal for revising it. There may even be situations where a speaker or writer believes himself to be doing the former when he is unwittingly doing the latter.

In Chapter 5 we shall argue that operant psychology involves a series of proposals for conceptual revision.

It is important to bear in mind that conceptual issues can arise not only in science but also in matters of law. Thus, in the case of (3a), although it is at present a trivial matter whether a tomato is classified as a fruit or as a vegetable, if in fact vegetables but not fruits became subject to a special new tax it would clearly be in the interests of tomato sellers to obtain a ruling that a tomato is a fruit. This, of course, is not just 'a dispute over words', though a discussion about the meaning of the word 'vegetable' is part of what is involved. A court of law, however, does not simply make an arbitrary decision; if it had to decide a matter of this sort it would have to take a number of factors into account, including past rulings and relevant similarities and differences. Flew (1951, pp. 3–4) cites a case which involved a dispute as to whether or not a flying boat counted as a 'ship'; and one can see how it would be open to one counsel to point out the similarities between flying boats and ships in the standard sense and to the other counsel to point out the differences. The final ruling was in fact that a flying boat is *not* a ship. Wittgenstein has noted that uncertainty where boundary lines come is not necessarily due to ignorance, since in some cases 'We do not know the boundaries because none have been drawn' (1953, section 69). It follows, of course, that the answer to any question of the form 'Is an X a Y?' may sometimes be 'Yes and no', since Xs may be like standard cases of Y in some respects and not in others. When all the similarities and differences are agreed there can be no further argument, and in these situations one needs to bear in mind a further dictum of Wittgenstein (1953, section 79), viz. 'Say what you like, as long as it does not stop you from seeing how things are.' It is important to note, however, that he then adds: 'And when you have seen this there is plenty that you will *not* say.'

This 'say-what-you-like' formula is one to which we shall be returning in later chapters, since there are many conceptual issues in psychology where it is applicable. In the meantime it may be helpful for purposes of illustration to cite an example from a different area in the philosophy of science. There are obvious pressures from astronomy which indicate that 'The earth goes round the sun' is a more helpful statement than 'The sun goes round the earth'. It does not follow, however, that it is merely foolish or obscurantist to prefer the latter: the person who says this may simply be making an intentional choice to continue to use the sense of 'going round' to which he has been accustomed; and if he is interested, for instance, in siting the windows of his house he will not be misled. It would, of course, be quite a different matter if he were in charge of organizing a journey into space. The great merit of the 'say-what-you-like' formula is its recognition that a form of words may be adequate in one context and not in another. On this showing, an appropriate answer to the question, 'Does the sun *really* go round the earth?' is 'Yes and no'; and as long as one has appreciated all the reasons for saying 'yes' and all the reasons for saying 'no' there is nothing more to discuss.

In lighter vein, here is a masterly description of the reactions of some 11-year-olds to the conceptual claim that 'mathematics is a language'.

> 'A language! You mean they actually talk in it?'
>
> 'Well, not people like *us*, perhaps. But learned professors and old geezers like that can understand one another in maths, even if they don't all speak English'.
>
> The idea of mathematics as a language was something that Temple found hard to resist. He gave Martin-Jones a friendly punch in the ribs and said: 'I say, let's be two learned professors talking in maths'.
>
> 'Righto'. Martin-Jones took up his cue and spoke in tones of bogus importance. 'Good morning, Professor Temple! $a^2 + 2ab + b^2$, don't you think?'. . .
>
> 'Sir, please, sir, can you speak maths, sir?'
>
> Mr Wilkins paused in the act of reaching for the chalk. 'Can I speak *what*?'
>
> 'Darbishire says mathematics is a language. He's bonkers, isn't he, sir?'
>
> 'So it is a language, in a way', Mr Wilkins agreed. 'It's a means of communication'.
>
> Temple was interested. 'Wow! Would you say something in mathematics, please, sir? Say "Good afternoon, it's a lovely day to-day" in algebra!'
>
> Mr Wilkins *tut-tutted* in despair. 'You silly little boy! You can't say things like that'.
>
> 'No?' Temple sounded disappointed. 'Well, in that case it isn't really a language, is it, sir?' (From *Leave it to Jennings* by Antony Buckeridge, Collins, 1963, pp. 77–8 and 105)

This is a typical 'yes-and-no' situation; and on those occasions where we have reservations about whether X is a Y we sometimes say that it is not a 'genuine case of Y', is not 'strictly speaking a case of Y', 'is not a Y in the full sense', or (like Temple in the above passage) 'is not really a Y'.

Now it is sometimes suggested that philosophers are arrogant and dogmatic people who announce that it is *forbidden* to talk in certain ways. There is nothing necessarily arrogant, however, in commending fresh classifications or proposing that new boundaries should be drawn, and unless such proposals are made without giving supporting reasons it seems scarcely fair to make accusations of dogmatism. Often, too, it may simply be that after taking seriously a particular argument one no longer *wishes* to talk in certain ways; and it may even be possible that those who none the less persist in such talk have failed to see the force of the argument in question.

In many cases conceptual analysis involves making a comparison between sentences which are grammatically similar but logically different. Thus 'Tame tigers growl' is grammatically similar to 'Tame tigers exist', since both sentences contain adjective, noun, and verb. The two are logically different, however, since 'Some tame tigers growl and some do not' is an intelligible sentence, whereas 'Some tame tigers exist and some do not' is a logically impossible combination of words. Similarly, 'There is no such entity as "public opinion" ' is grammatically akin to 'There are no such things as centaurs'; but whereas the latter is an empirical matter and relates to what one will or will not discover after searching, the former does not involve searching at all but is a statement about the interchangeability of concepts. A particularly helpful notion in this connection—and one which will play an important part in the present book—is that of 'translation'. We are thinking here not of translation in the familiar sense, in which one translates from, say, French into English, but of transformation of a particular expression into one which is logically equivalent. Thus those who assert that there is no such entity as 'public opinion' are in effect making the conceptual claim that sentences purporting to be about public opinion require translation. For example, 'Public opinion has veered round in support of the Prime Minister' would need on this view to be rewritten as 'There are more people who now believe in the Prime Minister's policy than there were previously'. Mabbott (1947, pp. 151–152), from whom we have taken this example, says: 'The work of "analysis" consists not of analysing a non-existent entity but of rewriting the sentences so that the misleading subject is replaced by real subjects.' Similar translation would be needed of sentences about the growth of inflation or changes in fashion.

We suggested earlier that conceptual statements did not carry any predictions as a result of which their truth or falsity could be straightforwardly checked. This now needs qualification. If we look at our data in new ways we are often enabled to make sense of other facts which hitherto had seemed quite separate. To quote a well-known example, the concept of *attraction* exhibits the relationship between two such apparently disparate facts as the falling of an apple from a tree and the movement of tides. (There is a particularly interesting discussion of this example in Berkeley, *Principles of Human Knowledge*, sections

103–105.) In addition, however, if we take seriously a particular concept–for instance that of *attraction*—we may well be able to discover facts additional to those which we knew already. Conceptual proposals are thus not unrelated to particular facts, since the more new facts we discover and the more sense we are able to make of those facts which we already know, the greater our degree of confidence that the conceptual proposal which led to the discoveries is a helpful one. A particular perspective or approach is seldom decisively refuted by a single experiment, but if experimental results continue to be indecisive or uninteresting that approach tends gradually to be abandoned, while in other cases a concept turns out to be so important that it gains universal acceptance. Thus the phrenologists' concept of *philoprogenitiveness* has been entirely abandoned, whereas the concept of *natural selection* is never called in question. Breakthroughs in the history of science are regularly associated with conceptual innovation.

To bring out further the difference between conceptual and empirical statements it may be helpful to consider the ways in which each can be wrong. In the case of empirical statements the matter is straightforward. Thus a person might make the empirical claim that it is raining and be mistaken. (There would, of course, be a conceptual problem if there were just occasional drops and one was unsure if this would really count as 'raining', but this kind of problem arises in any situation where there are marginal cases.) Similarly a person can be wrong over the empirical generalizations which he makes. For example, in criticizing a colleague's research one does not normally dispute the particular facts which he claims to have discovered, since in most contexts one assumes that he has not miscalculated or misreported, but it may sometimes be possible to put forward alternative explanations of the same facts and thus show that some of his generalizations are faulty.

Disagreement over conceptual issues, however, may sometimes be a more complex affair. Here, for illustration purposes, is a homely example. A kindly lady was introduced to a very young child. She asked his age, and on hearing that he was 3 years old she said, 'He isn't 3 years old; he is 3 years young.' We call this example homely because the statement 'He is 3 years young' is unlikely to make people's hackles rise as do many conceptual statements about the merits of behaviourism, linguistic philosophy, etc. In other respects, however, it is a typical conceptual statement: it predicts nothing about the behaviour of clocks or calendars which is not also predicted by 'He is 3 years old' and does not contradict the latter in the way in which 'He is 4 years old' contradicts it. Like many other conceptual statements it involves a proposal that one should talk differently—not, of course, for aesthetic or stylistic reasons but because in talking differently one is thereby viewing the situation differently: this particular proposal invites one to reflect carefully on what standards can reasonably be expected from a child aged 3. In agreeing with such a conceptual statement, therefore, one is likely to use such expressions as 'Yes, that fits', or 'Yes, I see what you mean'. If one disagrees, it is because one rejects the proposed 'view' of the situation. In the present case one might wish to oppose what one regarded as 'mollycoddling' of 3-year-olds, and in that case one's reply to 'He is 3 years young' might be, 'Fiddlesticks! The sooner he learns to behave like a rational human being the better!'

Sometimes conceptual disagreements can be serious and bitter. For example, if X believes that Y's way of viewing a situation is wrong he is likely also, at least some of the time, to be opposed to Y's practices; and if Y has made it his life's work to promote such practices it is scarcely surprising, simply from a consideration of the logic of the situation, that heated discussion should sometimes follow. Clarification of what the dispute is about—and especially the distinguishing of conceptual issues from empirical ones—can sometimes do something to ease the tension, but if X commends a particular view of a situation and Y commends a different view one cannot as a matter of logic expect that either reasoned argument or appeal to evidence will necessarily give decisive grounds for preferring the one to the other. It is perhaps worth adding that where there is disagreement over fundamentals a common result is likely to be misperception of what conceptual proposals one's 'opponent' (as one sees him) is making. Sometimes, therefore, there is misunderstanding as well as disagreement, along with the irritation of feeling that the 'opponent' has not taken the elementary trouble of finding out what one is trying to say. It is our experience that some of the criticisms of both Freud and Skinner have been based on such misunderstanding; and in general it is of course unprofitable to argue about the merits of conceptual proposals whose significance one has misunderstood.

There are also situations where a person can be wrong in asserting that certain concepts are interchangeable. For example, if he were to assert that statements of the form 'A is the cause of B' are always equivalent to statements of the form 'Whenever an event of type A occurs it is regularly followed by an event of type B', someone else might show, by producing counter examples, that this equivalence did not always hold. In general, it is not impossible to challenge conceptual statements, but disagreements about them are in important ways quite different from disagreements on empirical matters. Those who profess to disagree with a particular conceptual proposal are in effect saying that the alleged new 'insight' is misguided or inappropriate, that it emphasizes the wrong things at the expense of the right ones, or simply that the concepts in question do not in fact function in the way described.

Many of the statements in this book will be conceptual in character, though we shall not hesitate to make empirical and other kinds of claim where these seem relevant. In addition we shall at times be pointing out that particular issues are or are not empirical or conceptual—a procedure which can in effect be regarded as a 'higher-order' type of conceptual discussion. In general the book can be regarded as an exercise in second-order psychology or 'meta-psychology', i.e. a critical examination of some of the concepts used by psychologists (and by operant psychologists in particular) in the course of their research. We shall try to show that conceptual errors not only generate unnecessary disputation and false inferences but may actually lead psychological research in unprofitable directions. In the next chapter we shall set out some of the techniques by means of which such errors can be detected.

Chapter 3

Conceptual Analysis and Conceptual Revision

It was pointed out in the last chapter that many conceptual issues hinge on the question of whether an X should count as or be classified as a Y—whether a flying boat should count as a ship, for instance, or whether a tomato should count as a vegetable. Those conceptual statements which involve reference to existing boundaries were said to be examples of 'conceptual analysis', while those conceptual statements which call for the redrawing of boundaries were said to be examples of 'conceptual revision'. It was also pointed out that conceptual revision can occur either by the invention of a new word or by the stipulation that an existing word should be used in a new way.

Now whether one's intention is to analyse concepts or to revise them, in either case it is necessary to consider what philosophers have called the 'ordinary use' of words. Since this phrase has given rise to misunderstanding some clarification seems called for as to why 'ordinary use' has been considered important.

It needs to be emphasized in the first place that philosophical discussion in this area is not concerned with any kind of survey of people's speech habits. Indeed, even if these habits were entirely changed this would not make any difference to the logical behaviour of the concepts involved. Thus, to take an extreme case, even if people consistently used the word 'some' where now we use the word 'all' and vice versa, this would make no difference to the logical behaviour of the concepts now expressed by the words 'some' and 'all'; it would mean only that we had to interchange the two words in talking about this behaviour. Some years ago one of the authors was present at a discussion in which an outraged professor of philosophy attempted to meet objections to his thesis by saying, 'I don't care tuppence if that is not how bus conductors talk.' This is good repartee but is unlikely to have disposed of the objection. Surveys can, of course, provide many interesting empirical truths: they indicate, for instance, what are the differences between spoken and written English; they can reveal the extent to which people speak grammatically and fluently or the reverse, and they can indicate the number of people who, like Mr Jingle in *Pickwick Papers*, talk in short staccato bursts. Such results, however, would have no particular conceptual or philosophical significance. Those who study the logical behaviour of concepts are concerned not with speech habits but with distinctions and classifications. 'Our ordinary words', says Austin (1962, p.3), 'are much subtler in their uses, and mark many more distinctions, than philosophers have realised.'

When Austin speaks here of 'ordinary words' the intended contrast is presumably not between ordinary and technical use but between the use of a word for familiar and clearly defined purposes and its use in certain philosophical contexts where there has been some unwitting departure from existing methods of classifying. 'It disperses the fog', says Wittgenstein (1953, section 5), 'to study the phenomena of language in primitive kinds of application in which one can command a clear view of the aim and functioning of the words.' In another passage he says: 'When philosophers use a word . . . one must always ask oneself: is the word ever actually used in this way in the language-game which is its original home? What *we* do is to bring words back from their metaphysical to their everyday usage' (1953, section 116).

As a first example we should like to cite Austin's comments on the philosophical expression 'directly perceive'.

1. First of all, it is essential to realise that here the notion of perceiving *in*directly wears the trousers—'directly' takes whatever sense it has from the contrast with its opposite: while 'indirectly' itself (a) has a use only in special cases, and also (b) has *different* uses in different cases—though that doesn't mean, of course, that there is not a good reason why we should use the same word. We might, for example, contrast the man who saw the procession directly with the man who saw it *through a periscope*; or we might contrast the place from which you can watch the door directly with the place from which you can see it only *in the mirror*. Perhaps we might contrast seeing you directly with seeing, say, your shadow on the blind; and *perhaps* we might contrast hearing the music directly with hearing it relayed outside the concert-hall. However, these last two cases suggest two further points.

2. The first of these points is that the notion of not perceiving 'directly' seems most at home where, as with the periscope and the mirror, it retains its link with the notion of a kink in *direction*. It seems that we must not be looking *straight at* the object in question. For this reason seeing your shadow on the blind is a doubtful case; and seeing you, for instance, through binoculars or spectacles is certainly not a case of seeing you *indirectly* at all. For such cases as these last we have quite distinct contrasts and different expressions—'with the naked eye' as opposed to 'with a telescope', 'with unaided vision' as opposed to 'with glasses on'. (These expressions, in fact, are much more firmly established in ordinary use than 'directly' is.)

3. And the other point is that, partly no doubt for the above reason, the notion of indirect perception is not naturally at home with senses other than sight. With the other senses there is nothing quite analogous with the 'line of vision'. The most natural sense of 'hearing indirectly', of course, is that of being *told* something by an intermediary—a quite different matter. But do I hear a shout indirectly, when I hear the echo? If I touch you with a bargepole, do I touch you indirectly? Or if you offer me a pig in a poke, might I

feel the pig indirectly—*through* the poke? And what smelling indirectly might be I have simply no idea! (Austin, 1962, pp. 15–17; reproduced by permission of Oxford University Press)

Now it is no part of Austin's argument to suggest that ordinary use should never be changed. In effect, however, he is inviting his audience to become more sensitive to the many distinctions and nuances which are to be found if we study language with care; and, perhaps more important, he is suggesting, at least by implication, that lack of such care can result in downright bad philosophy. The danger, in his view, is not in conceptual innovation as such but in unwitting innovation, since this can result in false contrasts and misleading analogies.

This is a point to which we shall return later in this chapter, when we shall cite examples of the kinds of insight which the techniques of conceptual analysis can achieve. Before doing so, however, it may be helpful, particularly to readers unfamiliar with work in this area, if we say more about the techniques themselves. It is admittedly somewhat unsatisfactory to give 'potted versions' of philosophical methods which have taken many years to evolve, but at the risk of oversimplification we should like to offer three rules of thumb which can be used in a variety of ways whenever the logical behaviour of concepts is under discussion. The rules in question are: (a) apply Wittgenstein's 'polar principle'; that is to say, ask what is being *excluded*; (b) ask what would count as a *paradigm case* of the correct application of a concept; and (c) where a general statement is made, ask it it is true *in a particular case*.

(a) Since concepts distinguish, they divide material in at least a two-fold way. Thus if one characterizes something as being 'X' one is thereby excluding the thesis that it is 'not-X'. As an exercise the reader may like to consider what is excluded by the following terms: *higher, graduate, slow, bachelor, forgetful*. It makes no sense to speak of a distinction which does not distinguish anything, and if a person is said to understand a concept this implies that he also understands what is being excluded; indeed one cannot group without excluding as well as including.

The polar principle, then, invites us to ask the question, 'As opposed to what?' When confronted with a particular statement, there may be contexts— and, as will be seen, they are often highly sophisticated ones—where it is profitable to ask the speaker, 'What exactly is being excluded?' or 'What would it be like if you were wrong?'

This must not be taken simply as a request that the speaker should clarify his meaning. If this were so, the need to invoke the polar principle would disappear if only people expressed themselves clearly! It may indeed be true that an obscure statement may become less obscure if one has worked out what would be involved if its opposite were the case; but there is more to the polar principle than this: one could perhaps describe it as a device for exhibiting to a sophisticated thinker that there is something odd or paradoxical about what he is saying.

It is difficult to give examples which are not controversial; but for present purposes it is perhaps more important to find a 'live' issue where the polar principle can be applied than to avoid complications or controversy. With this requirement in mind, therefore, let us consider the thesis that *man is merely a highly complicated kind of machine*. To apply the polar principle in this case would be to invite the defender of this thesis to consider standard uses of 'machine' and 'mechanical' and to ask himself what it would be like *not* to be a machine. 'As things are', we might say to him, 'there are two words, "man" and "machine", both of which we know how to use appropriately. By the same token we can distinguish those situations where a person responds, as we say, "mechanically", e.g. by saying "Yes, yes" in a monotonous voice, from those situations where his responses are not mechanical. Are you then saying that responses which we thought were not mechanical are really mechanical after all? In that case, please indicate what characteristics a response would have to have for you to be justified in saying that it was *not* mechanical.'

Here is a second example. The evidence from psychotherapy suggests, or is believed to suggest, that the same defence mechanisms and the same apparently neurotic weaknesses are to be found in seemingly healthy people as are found in neurotic people. It immediately becomes tempting to say that 'really' (whatever this means) we are *all* neurotic. To apply the polar principle in this case would be to ask, 'What, then, is it like *not* to be neurotic?' This last example is controversial for a variety of reasons. There would of course be no logical objection to saying that all of us show signs of neuroticism some of the time, and there is the further complication that the word 'neurotic' is 'open-textured' (cf. p.13) in the sense that there are no precise formulated rules as to what exactly shall count as 'being neurotic'. For our purposes, however, the example is convenient: it is a live one (since many readers will be aware of the pressures which might lead a psychotherapist to say, 'We are all neurotic') and it exhibits an important characteristic of the polar principle, viz. that it is used as a way of critically examining certain claims which arise when knowledge has reached a certain degree of sophistication.

Now those who say that man is merely a machine and those who say that we are all neurotic are clearly making claims which are intended to be exciting and important. One function of the polar principle, however, is to exhibit the possibility that there is something deceptive in this challenge. Words, as we have already indicated, hunt in pairs, and if one member of the pair correctly occurs in a sentence it is at least meaningful, even if false, that the other member should be substituted. In these two examples, however, it is impossible as a matter of logic that any such substitution should occur, since the familiar distinctions between 'man' and 'machine' and between 'neurotic' and 'normal' are being disallowed. The words 'machine' and 'neurotic' are thus both being used without a polar term, which means that no distinction is being drawn.

To employ a term in common use among philosophers, use of the word 'neurotic' is *parasitic* upon there being a distinction between 'neurotic' and 'normal'. Unless we were aware of such a distinction the claim that we are all neurotic could not startle us in the way that it does. In general, the use of one member of a pair of terms is parasitic upon there being a polar or contrasting term; and if no such contrast is intended then the use of the original term is misleading. In this particular case, if one met a paradigm case of a normal person and someone said that he, too, was neurotic, one could rightly ask, 'What in that case does "normal" mean?' Indeed, if there had never been any grounds for distinguishing neurotic from normal behaviour, then it is impossible as a matter of logic that anyone would ever have learned to use the word 'neurotic' correctly. From the fact that plenty of people *have* learned to use the 'normal–neurotic' distinction correctly, however, it follows that there must have been grounds—even if not satisfactory ones—for initially making it. In applying the polar principle, therefore, one is in effect asking people to reflect on some initial distinction.

On this showing, of course, the passage from Austin, quoted above, is an example of skilful use of the polar principle: he was offering a challenge to those philosophers who spoke of 'direct perception' to say what *indirect* perception would involve.

(b) The second 'rule of thumb' is that one should consider how a concept is used in a so-called 'paradigm case', i.e. in a typical or standard case where it is correctly applied; one can then see the extent to which a new situation where this concept is used approximates to the standard. For example, if a person smiles and makes welcoming remarks to a stranger, then—provided the context is such that no hypocrisy is involved—this is a situation *par excellence* where one would be entitled to say that the person was *friendly*. The concept of *friendliness* entails precisely such behaviour, and to be friendly just *is* to act in these or similar ways. It makes sense to doubt whether a person regularly so behaves, but if he does it would be impossible as a matter of logic to deny that he was friendly. Indeed, if someone attempted to deny this one's rejoinder might well be, 'If that is not being friendly then I do not know what "being friendly" means.' Similarly if one met a paradigm case of a normal person and someone said that he, too, was neurotic, one could rightly ask, 'What in that case does "normal" mean?'; and if one met what was manifestly a human being and was told that he was a machine, one could legitimately say, 'If this person is not a human being then I do not know what "human being" means.'

(c) The third 'rule of thumb' may be formulated as follows: to bring out what is involved by a statement one should consider a particular consequence and ask if this is what the speaker intends. Even before the time of Wittgenstein this technique had been systematically used by G. E. Moore as a way of exhibiting the oddity of some of the things which were being said by his philosophical contemporaries (see, for instance, Moore, 1959, especially pp.32–59). If we now try to follow Moore's lead in the case of our present two examples, the argument would be: 'You say that man is merely a machine. It follows, therefore, that this is true of *all* men. In that case, let us consider the particular man, Smith, and ask if *he* is a machine.' Similarly it might be argued: 'You say that we are *all* neurotic. Let us begin by asking you to justify your implied claim that Smith is neurotic.'

It is not, of course, being suggested that general statements as a class are vulnerable in this way. Thus there is nothing self-defeating in saying that all human adults are over 3 feet tall. In this case we know exactly what is being excluded, and there would be no temptation whatsoever, if we found a person under 3 feet tall, to say that 'really' he was over 3 feet after all. The technique which we have described is applicable only when standard cases of being an X are in some way being disallowed.

What has been said so far, however, does not do justice to the full complexity of our two examples. If it did, one could reject both 'Man is merely a complicated machine' and 'We are all neurotic' as mere blunders or aberrations, which clearly they are not. It is possible, however, to reinterpret them by saying that each is in effect a proposal for conceptual innovation. On this showing what is involved is a plea for the abandonment of a distinction—in the one case the distinction between human nervous systems and artefact 'nervous systems', in other case the distinction between 'normal' and 'neurotic' responses in a therapy situation. It is not for us to defend either plea; but it is perhaps worth pointing out that distinctions can be useful in one context and not in another.

As a final illustration we should like to quote a remarkable passage from Hippocrates, in which he points out that in the classification of diseases a contrast between 'divine' and 'human' is unnecessary. After indicating that the heart and diaphragm ('phrenes') 'have nothing to do . . . with the operations of the understanding' but that these involve the brain, he makes the following comments on epilepsy:

> The disease called the Sacred arises from causes as the others, namely those things which enter and quit the body, such as cold, the sun, and the winds which are ever changing and never at rest. And these things are divine, so that there is no necessity for making a distinction, and holding this disease to be more divine than the others, but all are divine and all human.' (From *The Genuine Works of Hippocrates*, tr. F. Adams, London, 1894, vol. II, p. 857)

This is a quite remarkable anticipation of the polar principle!

Our next task will be to cite some further examples of the way in which the above philosophical techniques can be used. These examples will, we hope, be ones which psychologists can recognize as relevant to some of their own theoretical problems. Our intention, however, is not to try to solve all the philosophical questions raised, but simply to give the reader the chance to see the techniques in action and thus have a preview of the use to which they will be put later in this book.

In the left-hand column we have therefore set out a series of statements in which certain key words have what Wittgenstein would call a 'metaphysical' usage, while in the right-hand column we exhibit the same words when they are used 'in the language-game which is [their] original home'. Our purpose is not to make claims about the truth or appropriateness of either class of statement but only to set them out side by side so as to exhibit the differences.

'Metaphysical' usage	*Usage in 'original language-game'*
(1) 'We can never really know that there is a table in front of us.'	'Are you quite sure there is a table in your study?'
(2) 'We can never study learning itself (or intelligence or memory or attitudes), only their outward manifestations.'	'I know that clocks tick and strike and that their hands move, but I know nothing about the mechanisms inside.'
(3) 'Sensations are the raw data on which our perceptions are built.'	'I was aware of strange sensations'; 'I felt a tingling sensation in my toe'; 'This house is built of brick.'
(4) 'My toothache is private to me.'	'This road is private.'
(5) 'You cannot step twice into the same river.'	'Is this the Ouse again? If so, I paddled in it yesterday.'

Now it is worth noting at the outset that the statements on the left become important only after we have reached a certain degree of sophistication. (1), for example, is a *sceptical* conclusion in the sense that it seems to imply some kind of limitation to human knowledge. Yet, as Berkeley pointed out, the plain man is in no danger of being worried by such alleged limitations. 'We see the illiterate bulk of mankind that walk the high road of plain common sense . . . for the most part easy and undisturbed . . . They complain not of any want of evidence in their senses, and are out of all danger of becoming sceptics' (*Principles of Human Knowledge*, Introduction, section 1).

Problems arise, in Berkeley's view, only in more learned types of discussion.

> Bid your servant meet you at such a *time*, in such a *place*, and he shall never stay to deliberate on the meaning of these words: in conceiving that particular time and place, or the motion by which he is to get thither, he finds not the least difficulty. But if *time* be taken, exclusive of all those particular actions and ideas that diversify the day, merely for the continuation of existence, or duration in the abstract, then it will perhaps gravel even a philosopher to comprehend it. (*Principles of Human Knowledge*, Part I, section 97)

Berkeley was aware that apparently sceptical conclusions are not always the result of 'the obscurity of things, or the natural weakness and imperfection of our understandings' (*Principles of Human Knowledge*, Introduction, section 2). Often what is involved is *unnecessary* disputation because in a subtle way we have been hoodwinked by words. 'We have first raised a dust, and then complain, we cannot see' (*Principles of Human Knowledge*, Introduction, section 3).

Indeed (2), like (1), is just the kind of sceptical claim against which Berkeley's argument might have been directed. 'What you call the empty forms and outside of things', says Philonous, 'seems to me the very things themselves' (*Third Dialogue between Hylas and Philonous*). To put Berkeley's point in another way, there is a difference between the situation where one is genuinely looking at outward manifestations, e.g. the moving of the hands of a clock in contrast with the moving of the cog wheels inside, and the situation where no such contrast is involved. Similarly, to apply the same kind of argument to (2), if a person claims to be studying learning or intelligence or memory or attitudes it is gratuitous to suppose that, lying behind or beyond what he observes, is something else which no one could ever conceivably observe, and that it is these hidden things to which the words 'learning', 'intelligence', 'memory', and 'attitude' refer; and it follows that the sceptical lament that such entities are for ever beyond the reach of our knowledge is unjustified. It is true, of course, that on the basis of a subject's responses it is possible in principle to make inferences to events inside his body, just as one might make inferences about the mechanisms of a clock from studying the movements of its hands. Any statements made on the basis of such inferences, however, would be physiological in character, whereas it is plain that the concepts *learn, remember, intelligent* and *attitude* have been correctly applied through the ages by people who knew none of the relevant physiology; it follows, therefore, that if one is using these terms in their ordinary sense nothing physiological is predicted by them.

It is, of course, open to an innovator to use such terms in a new way; for example, if it were found that in all situations where a subject could be said to have learned something a particular physiological statement, e.g. about changes occurring at the synapse, were always true, there would be a case for saying that learning was 'really' a set of changes occurring at the synapse. This, however, would involve an innovation and would not be a correct account of the word 'learn' as it is at present understood. In point of fact the search for the 'real' nature of learning or the 'real' meaning of the word 'learn' is almost certainly misguided. It is a mistake, as Berkeley pointed out, to suppose 'that every name hath, or ought to have, one only precise and settled signification' (*Principles of Human Knowledge*, Introduction, section 18). The same point is emphasized by Wittgenstein, who cites as an example the word 'game'.

Don't say: 'There *must* be something common, or they would not be called 'games'—but *look and see* whether there is anything common to all.—For if you look at them you will not see something that is common to *all*, but similarities, relationships, and a whole series of them at that. To repeat: don't think but look!—Look for example at board-games, with their multifarious relationships. Now pass to card-games; here you find many correspondences with the first group, but many common features drop out, and others appear. When we pass next to ball games, much that is common is retained, but much is lost.—Are they all 'amusing'? Compare chess with noughts and crosses. Or is there always winning and losing, or competition between players? Think of patience. In ball games there is winning and losing; but when a child throws his ball at the wall and catches it again, this feature has disappeared. Look at the parts played by skill and luck; and at the difference between skill in chess and skill in tennis. Think now of games like ring-a-ring-a-roses; here is the element of amusement, but how many other characteristic features have disappeared! And we can go through the many, many other groups of games in the same way; can see how similarities crop up and disappear.

He concludes that: 'We see a complicated network of similarities overlapping and criss-crossing . . . I can think of no better expression to characterise these similarities than "family resemblances" ' (Wittgenstein, 1953, sections 66–67).

By the same argument, therefore, it is not necessarily correct to suppose that those situations where someone is said to have learned something will all have some single characteristic in common; on the contrary there may be a variety of 'family resemblances'. The same may also be true in the case of those situations where a person remembers something, displays intelligence, or exhibits a hostile attitude. It is a mistake in the first place to assume that there is always some unique defining characteristic, and it is doubly mistaken to suppose that the events which we observe are in some way outward manifestations of some 'inner' occurrence which constitutes the 'real' meaning of the words 'learn', 'remember', 'intelligence', and 'attitude'. In some contexts, as Wittgenstein points out, it may be helpful to ask what particular *examples* taught us the meaning of a word, since in that case 'it will be easier for you to see that the word must have a family of meanings' (1953, section 77).

Examples (3) and (4) are, we believe, self-evident without detailed discussion. It is sufficient to point out that, in the left hand column, the familiar words 'sensation' and 'private' when used in this sophisticated context have undergone a subtle change of meaning.

With regard to (5), the claim that one cannot step twice into the same river is attributed to the Greek thinker, Heraclitus, and is believed to have been part of his general emphasis on the phenomena of *change*. The statement is an interesting one because, if taken literally, it is manifestly false, since one might step into the Ouse at 10 in the morning and again at 12 noon. If Heraclitus then answered that in that case it was no longer the same river, he would in effect be saying that there are no situations where one is entitled to speak of 'the same river' or indeed entitled to use the word 'same' at all. The polar term to 'same' is 'different', use of the one being parasitic on use of the other; and we might therefore interpret Heraclitus as saying that in a true account of the world this pair of terms would not be needed.

Now the fact that one can formulate correct sentences in the right-hand column does not establish that the sentences in the left-hand column are simply blunders. What it establishes is the existence of *differences*. To try, for example, to infer the nature of learning from a study of people's behaviour is in important ways *unlike* inferring the mechanisms of a clock from the movements of its hands. Similarly, to say 'You cannot step twice into the same river' is in an important respect *unlike* saying 'You cannot step twice into the Ouse'. If the speaker has not noticed the difference he is misleading himself, and once he has seen 'how things are' (cf. p. 15) he may decide that he no longer wishes to talk in that way.

There may be occasions, however, where the conceptual claim is made with full awareness of its implications. For example, a person who says 'We can never really know that there is a table in front of us' might defend his statement in some such way as this: 'I quite admit that in the ordinary sense of "know" it is correct to say that we sometimes know that there is a table in front of us. But I am inviting you to change your standards of what constitutes knowledge.' He might plead, in support of this, that, in contrast with empirical truths, the truths of mathematics and logic have a special character of necessity or indubitability, and that this is the area where knowledge in the full sense is to be found. This is perhaps one of those philosophical questions to which the answer is 'yes and no' (cf. p.15); if one has seen all the reasons for revising our standards of what constitutes knowledge and all the reasons for keeping them as they are, then *ex hypothesi* there is nothing more to discuss.

To appeal to the ordinary use of words does not therefore commit one to saying that conceptual boundaries should never be changed; and indeed different investigators—legislators, physicists, psychologists, and many others—may need to reclassify for all kinds of different reasons. What is important is to be able to recognize revisionist proposals when one meets them. If one fails to appreciate that a particular word has undergone a shift in meaning one may fail to distinguish things which are different; and indeed psychology books at the present time all too often contain unwitting or unexamined proposals for conceptual innovation. To examine how a word functions 'in the language-game which is its original home' will not tell us what revisions ought to be made but it will force us to think carefully about what it is that we are revising.

Chapter 4

The Subject Matter of Psychology

> From colour-theories to defence-mechanisms, from the functions of a white rat's vibrissae to the mystic's sense of unutterable revelation, from imaginary playmates to partial correlations—wherein lies that unity of subject matter which leads us to speak, compactly enough, of 'contemporary psychology?' From behaviourism or *Gestalt* psychology to psychoanalysis or the objective measurement of character, the eye wanders over an interminable range of experiments, measurements, hypotheses, dogmas, disconnected facts, and systematic theories. (Murphy, 1932, p. 1)

So wrote Gardner Murphy in 1932; and although the quantity of psychological research which has been published since that time is truly formidable, it is still often believed, even in some cases by psychologists themselves, that the theoretical foundations of psychology are as controversial as they always were. Psychologists, it might be said, cannot even agree as to what psychology is.

We do not share this pessimism. We shall try to show in the present chapter that disputes about the subject matter of psychology can be regarded as *conceptual* in character; and from this it follows that the techniques discussed in Chapters 2 and 3 can be used to clarify—and in some cases even to resolve—the points of disagreement.

What psychology has lacked, until now, is a clearly defined method of arbitration; and we shall try to show that this is what conceptual analysis can supply. The situation can perhaps be compared with that described by Kant two centuries earlier:

> Metaphysics has accordingly lapsed back into . . . ancient time-worn dogmatism . . . And now, after all methods, so it is believed, have been tried and found wanting, the prevailing mood is that of weariness and complete *indifferentism*—the mother, in all sciences, of chaos and night, but happily in this case the source, or at least the prelude, of their approaching reform and restoration. (Kant, *Critique of Pure Reason*, Preface to first edition)

In what follows we shall try to show that it is possible in formulating the subject matter of psychology to pass beyond what Kant calls 'dogmatism' (or, as one might say, mere assertion and counter-assertion) to a position where the limits of rational enquiry can be clearly defined. In particular we hope to dispose, once and for all, of arguments about the merits and de-merits of behaviourism. This indeed is an area where 'dogmatism' has appeared at its worst: for the last 50 years behaviourism, with all kinds of variants, has been attacked, defended, dismissed, resuscitated, misunderstood and modernized, without any one view having received universal acceptance.

We shall consider a number of formulations which have been put forward in the attempt to answer the question, 'What is the subject matter of psychology?'; and we shall show how different formulations select different points for emphasis. In an important sense, therefore, one's choice of formula depends on what one regards as important, and alternative formulae can then be thought of as supplying corrective slants so that other features of the situation are not overlooked. In the last resort it is thus a case of 'say what you like' (cf. p.15), provided, of course, that one is fully aware of all the reasons for talking in one way rather than in another.

For convenience we shall group answers to the question 'What is the subject matter of psychology?' under five heads. These are *dualist theories, behaviourist theories, cluster theory, cybernetic theory*, and *operant theory*. We shall not attempt any detailed exposition of the views in question (since we assume that the reader will already be familiar with them), nor shall we attempt an exhaustive examination of the pros and cons of each. Our purpose is to show that if one recognizes that the issues are *conceptual* in character there is no longer any need to regard psychology as being bedevilled by insoluble controversies. Disagreements over classification and over emphasis are still possible and one may even sometimes be puzzled as to why one's colleagues wish to play a particular 'language-game'; but in most cases the pressures which encourage one form of talk and those which encourage a different form of talk can be recognized for what they are. The analogy with psychotherapy has been usefully exploited in this connection (see Wisdom, 1953; Farrell, 1946); one may remain philosophically 'neurotic' if the sources of the conceptual conflict are not made explicit, and suitable conceptual analysis, though at times it may 'cure' a person of wanting to talk in certain ways, is basically non-directive and is aimed rather at helping a person to be more effective in operating the conceptual scheme of his own choosing.

We do not use the word 'theory' in any proprietory sense. It is worth noting, however, that in some contexts what has been called a 'theory' is in effect a *conceptual formulation*. For example, supporters of Gestalt theory were implicitly—and indeed sometimes explicitly—attempting to exhibit the value of certain concepts, those, for instance, of *insight, Prägnanz*, and *isomorphism*; similarly supporters of psychoanalytic theory are at least implicitly proclaiming the value of concepts such as those of *projection, infantile sexuality*, and *unconscious mental processes*. By analogy, therefore, the five different types of answer to the question, 'What is the subject matter of psychology?' can correctly be called 'theories', though some less familiar expression, such as 'conceptual scheme', would have done as well.

We shall attempt to resolve outstanding disputes (in so far as this is possible) not by proclaiming that all psychologists ought to be dualists or behaviourists, nor even by proclaiming that they ought always to use operant concepts (an issue which will be discussed in Chapter 7), but by considering what conceptual stipulations or proposals are advantageous, or the reverse, for particular purposes.

Although the order in which we shall consider these five theories is approximately a chronological one (since behaviourism was a reaction against dualism and the cybernetic and operant approaches are both in an important sense developments from behaviourism), our choice of this order has in fact been determined by logical rather than chronological considerations. It is clearly necessary to consider dualism before one can discuss behaviourism, and it seemed desirable to indicate the diversity implied by cluster theory before considering the unity implied by the cybernetic and operant approaches. Any exact attention to chronology would in any case have been impossible since different and prima facie incompatible conceptual schemes were in fact existing side by side.

1. *Dualist theories*

The Cartesian formula of 'two kinds of substance' or 'two kinds of entity' is not wholly misleading (as some present-day thinkers perhaps suppose), and at the time when it was put forward was anything but unreasonable. Its particular merit is that it emphasizes that human beings, even though their bodily activity may be subject to mechanical laws, can none the less be initiators of action. Thus the experimenter in psychology *decides* how he wishes to present the stimuli, and although his actions can themselves be made the object of scientific study this does not alter the obvious empirical fact that such decisions take place, whatever the correct analysis of the concept of *deciding*. In addition dualism emphasizes that man is capable of consciousness: he can be aware, for instance, of the many wonderful colours and sounds in the world around him and indeed can be aware of his awareness. It is perhaps not altogether surprising, therefore, that the idea of 'happenings' in a different 'world' from that of ordinary 'physical objects' began to take shape; and although, as Ryle (1949, p. 199) has indicated, the idea of two—or any other number—of 'worlds' is uncomfortable in this context, a dualist view at least guarantees that the importance of consciousness is not overlooked.

In point of fact the word 'psychology' appears to have been very little used before the nineteenth century, and indeed it is hard to see how it could have come to be used at all in its present sense except in a context of post-Cartesian thinking. To the Greeks a 'psyche' was what made living objects alive: what is 'empsychon' ('be-souled') is capable of perception and capable of generating its own movement (see Aristotle, *De Anima*, 403 d), and St Paul (I Corinthians xv, 44–5) interestingly contrasts the 'psychikon soma', i.e. our ordinary living body, with a 'pneumatikon soma' (translated in the New English Bible as 'spiritual body' and perhaps to be thought of as the same person in some kind of renewed form). In the nineteenth century, however, it seems likely that most scholars would have been prepared to translate the word 'psyche' as 'soul', an entity to be contrasted with the body; and it was natural, therefore, to think of psychology as 'the study of the psyche'. Similarly it seemed appropriate to regard the so-called 'events of consciousness' (feelings of pain, awareness of colour, sound, etc.) as 'mental' or 'psychical' phenomena and to regard them as suitable objects for study no less than 'physical' phenomena.

This view persisted at least until the time of William James. Indeed, as we saw in Chapter 1, Fechner even claimed to be showing how the physical and psychical worlds were related. Freud, too, appears to have accepted uncritically the view that there was such a thing as the 'psychical apparatus', and even in more recent years psychoanalytic claims have been couched in dualist terms, Freud's achievement being characterized as 'the discovery of the unconscious mind' (cf. Miles, 1966, Chapter 6). Indeed, until the end of the nineteenth century and even later almost everybody who considered the matter appears to have assumed a basic duality between physical phenomena and mental phenomena and to have taken for granted that the task of psychology was either to study the latter or, in the case of psycho-physics, to study relationships between the two.

There are, of course, many words which in their original use implied a particular theoretical position, e.g. 'sunrise', 'hysteria' (a disease of the womb), 'jovial' (displaying a certain character through having been born under Jove), etc., but whose theoretical implications were later forgotten; and both 'psychology' and 'psycho-physics' belong in this class. The former is a particularly tiresome word, not only because it tends to be misunderstood (and considerable effort is therefore needed in explaining to laymen and prospective students what psychology is *not*) but because its theoretical implications are at least controversial: few psychologists nowadays would claim that in some literal sense they were studying an entity called the 'psyche'. In addition certain popular uses of the word 'psychological', e.g. 'a psychological case', gaining a 'psychological advantage' over one's opponent in sport, or adopting the right 'psychological approach' to invalids, employees, recalcitrant children, etc., may have misled even psychologists themselves, at any rate in so far as they feel that they have—or ought to have—special skills in such areas. This is as absurd as supposing that they are specially equipped to study performance at mental arithmetic rather than performance involving written calculations. We do not dispute that there may be good reasons for using the word 'psychological' in these popular senses, but there is a danger, as a result, that both psychologists and laymen will be led to expect expertise when there is none to be had. Certainly communication with invalids, employees, and recalcitrant children could be made (and has indeed been made) the subject of systematic research, but it is a mistake to hope that someone called a 'psychologist' will have special expertise on such matters before the research has even started! On theoretical grounds the case for abandoning the word 'psychology' is no doubt extremely strong; in practice, however, it has become so firmly entrenched that it seems less trouble to let it stand and simply discount the implication 'study of the psyche', just as one uses the word 'jovial' while discounting the implication 'born under Jove'.

Moreover it is important not to overlook that dualist theories correctly invite us to take seriously the *differences* between human beings on the one hand and animals and automata on the other. As we shall see, it is also possible to take these differences seriously in cluster theory, cybernetic theory, and operant theory; and there are in fact other ways of describing them than by saying that humans are non-physical substances or that experiences of joy or sorrow are events in a non-physical world. Indeed it is not easy to see why non-physical substances should be more deserving of reverence or respect than people. The differences are there, however; and it is perhaps fair to say that dualism in its traditional form is a misleading way of drawing attention to facts which are agreed to be important.

2. *Behaviourist theories*

Not all the claims made in the name of 'behaviorism' have been of the same logical type. Some of them were straightforwardly empirical, e.g. the claim that behaviour is influenced more by events which occur after conception than by genetic make-up, while some were concerned with research techniques, e.g. the claim that the method of introspection is of little value. Many of them, however, can be seen on inspection to be concerned with the logical behaviour of concepts.

It is possible to classify behaviourist claims into different types by examining the arguments by which they are supported. Traditionally, for example, behaviourist psychologists have been thought of as reluctant to study *instinctive* behaviour. But there are different reasons for such reluctance. Thus it would be possible without any absurdity for a psychologist to decide not to study instinctive behaviour simply on the grounds that he found it uninteresting. Alternatively he might decide that so little behaviour was in fact instinctive that there would not be enough material for a research programme; and this decision, being made on empirical grounds, would in principle be subject to revision if fresh data came to light or if existing data were reinterpreted. Finally, he might argue that the distinction between *instinctive* and *non-instinctive* behaviour serves no useful purpose, in which case anything which he studied would not be *called* 'instinctive behaviour'; and this would be a decision made on conceptual grounds. The policy issues, the empirical issues, and the conceptual issues are of course interrelated: empirical findings, for example, could well affect the conceptual decision as to whether the classification of behaviour into 'instinctive' and 'non-instinctive' was justified; but to say that the three issues are interrelated is not to say that they are indistinguishable.

Similarly, it is one thing to *advise against* the use of the method of introspection in research, on the grounds, for instance, that it produces inconsistent results between one subject and another, and quite a different thing to argue on conceptual grounds that because the word 'introspection' implies 'looking into the mind' *there cannot be such a thing*.

Now since there are different strands of meaning in the word 'behaviorism' it follows that there is no logical inconsistency in accepting some facets of behaviourism and rejecting others. Since words, in Wittgenstein's phrase, may have a 'family of meanings' (1953, section 77), it is unnecessary and misleading to hope to find the 'true' meaning of the word 'behaviourism'; and it follows that unless the different strands of meaning are distinguished it is not very profitable to proclaim oneself as being either 'for' or 'against'.

To examine these matters further, we shall make use of the grouping introduced by Mace (1948) into metaphysical, methodological, and analytical behaviourism. Briefly, the first of these views asserts that minds or mental events do not exist; the second claims that if they exist they are not suitable objects for scientific study, and the third claims that statements purporting to be about minds or mental events turn out on analysis to be statements about behaviour. We shall argue that discussions about the first two are the result of conceptual errors and that both acceptance and rejection are therefore equally unjustified, but that the third, analytical behaviourism, makes an important contribution to conceptual analysis.

We begin by considering a characteristic statement by J. B. Watson (1925, p.4): 'All psychology except behaviourism', he writes, 'is dualistic. That is to say we have both a mind (soul) and a body. This dogma has been present in human psychology from earliest antiquity.' Here the issue, at least at first glance, appears to hinge on a question of fact: either we have minds or we do not. If we do not, then a *materialist* view of human personality is correct and the ultimate reality is matter; if we do, then there exists something non-material in addition.

We shall argue, not that one of these views is right and the other wrong, but that discussion in these terms is the result of conceptual confusion.

At the start it is worth mentioning—so that it can be set on one side—the use of the word 'materialistic' in which it means 'concerned with material values'. In this sense people or societies are described as materialistic if they set special store by so-called 'material' goods—food and clothing, for example, and perhaps such things as cars and television sets—and have little interest in literature, art, and religion. In what follows we are not concerned with materialism in this sense, and still less have we any wish to defend it.

If, however, we consider the philosophical or metaphysical claim that 'nothing exists except matter', conceptual analysis immediately shows up its oddities. If it were an empirical claim, then certain differential predictions would follow. But what predictions could possibly be intended? No one disputes that people sometimes think, solve problems, remember things, day-dream, feel toothache, etc.; and if the reply is that when these things occur it is still the case that only material processes are involved, it is hard to see what 'material' could mean in this context; one can appropriately apply the polar principle and ask what would count as a paradigm case of something 'non-material'. Moreover, if no contrast is involved, how could anyone ever have learned the meaning of the word 'material' in this sense? (It is perhaps no accident that the word 'non-material' is seldom used outside philosophical contexts.) Quite apart from this it is not clear what sense has been given to the word 'exist'. One can ask if dodos still exist in Africa; one can be reminded of someone's existence by seeing his name in a newspaper, and one can ask if a number exists which satisfies certain specified conditions. None of these uses is applicable in the present context, however, and one is tempted to echo the words of Berkeley's Philonous who says: 'I am not for imposing any sense on your words: you are at liberty to explain them as you please. Only I beseech you, make me understand something by them' (*First Dialogue between Hylas and Philonous*). Statements containing the word 'exist' will be found on examination to be of a number of different logical types.

The thesis which Watson claims to be challenging, viz. that 'we have both a mind (soul) and a body', is grammatically similar to 'we have both a dog and a cat'. The latter, however, is clearly something which can be settled empirically, and if there were any controversy there is nothing which could not be resolved by a suitably thorough search. To discover whether we have minds or not, on the other hand, does not seem to be a matter of searching at all; and unless we are told what procedures are relevant we are simply being hoodwinked by words.

Here is a more recent claim (Beloff, 1962, p. 11) which appears to be in stark opposition to that of Watson but which is open to the same conceptual objections: 'The thesis of this book, if it can be stated in two words, is that Mind *exists*, or, to be more explicit, that minds, mental entities and mental phenomena exist as ultimate constituents of the world in which we live.'

Once again it is inappropriate to rush in either with agreement or with opposition. Beloff is at fault, in our view, not because he is mistaken in saying that minds exist when in fact they do not, but because he has failed to carry out the appropriate conceptual analysis.

Wittgenstein, as we have seen (1953, section 116), invites people, in the case of certain kinds of philosophical claim, to ask, 'Is the word ever actually used in this way in the language-game which is its original home?' One of the great difficulties in Beloff's thesis is that he has failed to give a use for the expression 'mind exists': it is simply not clear when we should ever want to use it. If someone says that Smith has an alert mind, it would be very strange for someone else to say, 'Yes, but at any rate his mind exists'; and if he proceeded to claim Smith's mind no longer existed or had never existed one might ask out of courtesy (if one wanted to try to understand him), 'Do you mean he is dead?' or 'Do you mean he has had a mental breakdown?' Clearly, however, it is not this sort of use which Beloff is considering; yet it is hard to see what other uses there could be. He admittedly warns his readers later in the book against those philosophers who try to stop people from asking important questions 'on the pretext that your question is "queer"' (Beloff, 1962, p. 258), but he seems to us to have failed to appreciate the logical 'queerness' of discussing minds in the way he does.

It is a mistake, then, to challenge Beloff's claim that minds exist with the counter-claim that they do not, and it is similarly mistaken to challenge Watson's claim that they do not with the counter-claim that they do. All such disputes seem to us to belong in the area of 'dogmatism' in Kant's sense. Unprofitable quasi-disputes of this kind can be avoided not by giving support to one side or to the other but by exhibiting the conceptual oddity of both claim and counter-claim.

It is possible, however, to put forward a somewhat more sophisticated version of materialism in which the conceptual nature of the issues is clearly recognized. On this showing it is the concepts of physics and chemistry which are in some way 'ultimate'. A materialist in this sense would not necessarily dispute that people can have feelings of pleasure in listening to fine music; he would claim, however, that in the last resort the music is a collection of amplitudes, frequencies, etc., and that the feelings of pleasure are in effect changes in the brain and therefore capable of being described in physico-chemical terms. It is hard to see, however, in what sense a conceptual scheme which has been found useful in physics and chemistry should be regarded as more 'ultimate' than any other conceptual scheme; and if it is suggested that the *real* world is that which contains the entities of physics and chemistry, it is questionable whether any sense has been given to the word 'real'. As Austin (1946, p. 159) has pointed out, if we speak of 'a real dog' this can often mean 'not a stuffed one', and if we speak of 'a real oasis' this would normally be taken to mean 'not a mirage', but when philosophers use the word 'real' it is not always clear what alternative is being excluded.

Perhaps we should also refer in passing to a more recent version of materialism, which has gained a serious following particularly in Australia. This is the so-called 'mind-brain identity thesis' by which mental events are said to be *identical with* brain events (see, for example, Armstrong, 1968; O'Connor, 1969). We shall not examine this view in any detail, though we must admit to some doubts as to whether the words 'identical with', as used in this context, can be given anything like their normal meaning. Certainly we are aware of no pressures from the point of view of operant psychology to adhere to this version of materialism; and indeed it is hard to see how the belief that mental states and brain states are identical—if indeed the supposition is a meaningful one in the first place—would encourage a practising psychologist or physiologist to do anything different from what he is doing already. To say this may be no more than an expression of personal interest; but in our experience there are so many 'live' conceptual issues arising directly from psychological research that we are hesitant to spend time on artificial issues generated by philosophers independently of any context in psychology or physiology.

Our conclusion is that a present-day psychologist need not profess to be a supporter of materialism or metaphysical behaviourism. This is not because some anti-materialist or anti-behaviourist counter-thesis is true but because the questions at issues are the product of conceptual confusion. In saying this we are not expressing a personal opinion: provided our conceptual analysis is correct the matter can be regarded as having been finally and decisively settled.

The pressures which led towards methodological behaviourism were of a different kind. Suitable recording techniques had made it possible to study changes of electrical potential in the brain; and it therefore seemed that by their use one might eventually hope to study the physiological correlates of all mental states. For example, if a deflection on a galvanometer is found to occur when a sharp stimulus impinges on the skin of an animal subject such as a cat, it is not unreasonable to suppose that one is studying the physiological correlates of the cat's feeling of pain. It became apparent, however, that although convincing evidence of physiological changes was possible at least in principle, definitive grounds for saying that the cat *felt pain* never seemed to be forthcoming! To argue that one can infer the cat's feelings of pain from its behaviour was considered to be unacceptable: if the only available evidence was the cat's behaviour—something which one could quite easily observe—it was quite unjustified to pretend to be making inferences to events which no one could ever observe. 'In 1912', writes Watson, 'the behaviourists reached the conclusion that they could no longer be content to work with intangibles and unapproachables' (1925, p. 6). Such a view did not necessarily imply that there were no such things as feelings of pain or other kinds of feeling, but only that such things were not proper objects for scientific study. Mental events were thus ruled out, not on the grounds that they did not exist but on grounds of methodological principle.

These alleged mental events came to be referred to as 'experiences'. Two apparently rival views therefore emerged: according to the one, psychology is the study only of behaviour; according to the other, it is the study not only of behaviour but of experience *in addition*.

The whole dispute, however, like disputes over materialism and metaphysical behaviourism, is the result of conceptual confusion. This confusion can be exhibited as follows. For purposes of argument let us suppose that someone has put forward the thesis, 'All that can be observed is behaviour.' Now instead of rushing in with professions of agreement or disagreement, it may turn out to be more helpful to apply the polar principle and ask him what it is which *cannot* be observed. If he then says that we can regularly observe behaviour but that we cannot observe other people's experiences, one can present him with a grammatically similar sentence, for example, that from one's window one regularly observes sparrows but never eagles, and invite him to consider the logical differences between this sentence and his original one. No one disputes that some things are hard to discover, whether because they are rare, like eagles, because they cannot easily be picked out, like the proverbial needle in a haystack, or indeed for some other reason. It is not this kind of difficulty, however, which prevents us from observing people's experiences. The word 'experience' is logically quite unlike, for instance, the word 'needle'. One might see or touch three needles, but it makes no sense to speak of seeing or touching any specified number of experiences nor to speak of lack of success in one's search for them; and the use of 'experience' and 'behaviour' as contrasting terms, as Farrell (1950) has shown, raises all kinds of difficulties. It follows that a methodological behaviourist is not a heartless individual who ignores people's feelings nor a narrow-minded individual who leaves out important areas of psychology; but he is a muddled individual who, like his putative opponent, is guilty of conceptual confusion. Once this confusion is exhibited there is nothing left to discuss, and the issue of methodological behaviourism can be finally laid to rest.

Analytical behaviourism is different from the other two versions of behaviourism in that its claims are unambiguously conceptual in character. Its central thesis is that sentences purporting to be about minds or mental events require translation into sentences about behaviour.

Many examples could be given where the proposed programme of translation is obviously correct. One is entitled to say, for instance, that a subject has learned something or remembers something if, after having previously been exposed to particular stimuli, he later behaves in certain ways. The suggestion here is not that psychologists *ought* to study behaviour as opposed to something else; it is that in studying behaviour in specifiable ways they are *thereby* doing psychology. There are admittedly difficulties in connection with concepts such as *mental image* and *toothache*—concepts to which we shall return on pp. 55–56; but there are undoubtedly many mentalistic concepts for which a behaviourist analysis is clearly applicable.

It does not, of course, follow on this view that psychologists should be doing anything different from what they are doing already but only that they should describe what they are doing in a different way. Behaviourism in this sense is a conceptual stipulation or proposal: it is neither a theory as to what is the case nor a set of instructions as to how to do research. Even the much criticized 'method of introspection' cannot be ruled out on conceptual grounds, whatever other reasons there may be for not using it; the most that an analytical behaviourist can say is that there should be a redescription of what is happening in terms of the subject's 'verbal report'.

The fact that a certain sentence admits of 'translation' does not, of course, mean that that sentence in its original form was false. For example, to say that the statement 'His mind was wandering' is a statement about behaviour has nothing to do with the question whether his mind was in fact wandering. Failure to appreciate this point has, we believe, misled both operant psychologists and their critics.

The case for analytical behaviourism was further strengthened by the arguments of Ryle (1949) when he pointed out that not all 'mentalistic' words, i.e. words such as 'know', 'see', 'sensation', 'intelligence', etc., stand for events or processes. Philosophers, so he suggested, had unwittingly assigned these words to incorrect 'categories' and thus generated unnecessary disputation. From his discussion of the word 'know', for example, it becomes immediately apparent that its logic is quite different from that of verbs which stand for activities, and to postulate recondite 'acts of knowing', therefore becomes unnecessary. His argument can, of course, be extended in many ways which are relevant to present-day psychology: thus the words 'remember', 'learn', 'recall', 'recognize', and 'forget' are none of them names of activities and *a fortiori* they are not names of activities taking place in a postulated 'mental world'. As has been pointed out on p. 38, we are misleading ourselves if we suppose that our research involves *inferring* these (unobserved) activities from observable behaviour.

We shall be returning to Ryle's argument several times during the course of this book. It would be an oversimplification to classify him in any straightforward way as an analytical behaviourist, but he shares with the analytical behaviourist the view that misconstruction of sentences containing mentalistic concepts has led to error.

Our own programme for psychology will in effect be an extension of that of analytical behaviourism, though our proposed 'programme of translation' relates not to mentalistic words as such but to words which are 'extra-episodic' in a sense to be explained in Chapter 6.

Before leaving the issue of behaviourism we should like to make two further comments. The first is to say something about the concept of *consciousness* (which in our view is quite a different concept from that of *mind*); the second is to show that, without a suitable conceptual analysis, even a distinguished investigator can make serious philosophical blunders.

(a) In discussions of behaviourism one often finds that the authors speak indiscriminately of 'mind' and 'consciousness' as though these two terms were more or less equivalent in function. If one considers carefully the 'language-games' in which they are used, however, it becomes plain that this is not so. 'Mental' can in some contexts be helpfully contrasted with 'physical', as when we speak of 'mental illness', and there are countless idioms which reflect human ability to operate with things which are not physically present: thus one speaks of 'mental' arithmetic when calculation is done without the use of marks on paper; one speaks of the 'psychological' effects of a drug or of a government proposal if one is considering what people will *believe* about the situation; one speaks of 'mental images' or a 'picture in the mind's eye' when what is imagined is not in fact present, and it is possible to be with somebody 'in spirit' even though one is many miles away. It is unnecessary, however, and (as some would say) 'ontologically uncomfortable', to suppose that this distinction commits one to a 'dualist' philosophical view involving belief in 'two kinds of reality, mental and physical'; one might as well profess to be a 'duodecimalist' because one believes that there are 12 months in the year! As has been pointed out already (Miles, 1963), the 'mental'–'physical' dichotomy is serviceable not because it marks some 'ultimate' distinction (whatever that means) but because it can be used to mark a series of much humbler distinctions.

The concept of *consciousness* is in many ways quite different. Like 'mental' and 'physical' it is sometimes mauled around uncritically by would-be philosophers, as in the expressions 'behaviour and consciousness' and 'conscious experience'. The former seems to imply that one might study behaviour on Mondays and consciousness on Tuesdays, while the latter seems to presuppose a contrast with 'unconscious experience'—an expression for which there does not appear to be any obvious use. For the most part, however, 'conscious' is not a philosophers' word at all: it is a serviceable everyday term, having such opposites as 'unconscious', 'asleep', and 'oblivious' whose use is not in dispute. On empirical grounds none of us doubts that a blow on the head can sometimes cause a person to lose consciousness, and if an anaesthetist was unable to tell whether a human being (or even an animal) was conscious he would soon lose his job. Nor do philosophical arguments cast any doubt on the claim that the emergence of consciousness is one of the most exciting things about man's evolution, and indeed any version of behaviourism which disputed this point would *ipso facto* not be worth taking seriously.

(b) Secondly, to support our claim that suitable conceptual analysis is needed if psychologists are to talk appropriately about the subject matter of psychology, we should like to quote a passage from Hebb's *Textbook of Psychology*, in which he offers an account of the nature of psychological enquiry.

> *Mind* and *mental* refer to the processes inside the head that determine the higher levels of organisation in behaviour . . . There are two theories of mind, speaking very generally. One is animistic, a theory that the body is inhabited by an entity—the mind or soul—that is quite different from it, having nothing in common with bodily processes. The second theory is physiological or mechanistic; it assumes that mind is a bodily process, an activity of the brain. Modern psychology works with this latter theory only. Both are intellectually respectable (that is, each has support from highly intelligent people, including scientists), and there is certainly no decisive means available of proving one to be right, the other wrong . . . Working with a particular theory is often on an 'as-if' basis, and does not require that the user should believe it. Saying that our knowledge of mind is theoretical rather than observational means that we study mind in the same way as a chemist studies the atom. Atoms are not observed directly, but their properties can be inferred from observable events. (Hebb, 1958, p. 3)

Now, in saying that the words 'mind' and 'mental' refer to 'processes inside the head', Hebb appears to have overlooked the elementary point that people have used mentalistic concepts for many centuries without having the least idea of what was going on inside the head. To say that someone is mentally alert, for instance, does not entail anything at all about events inside the head; and even if it came to be known that the mentally alert did in fact have certain physiological characteristics which distinguished them from the mentally non-alert, it would still not follow (unless one chose to make a major conceptual innovation) that 'mental alertness' *means* the having of those physiological characteristics. In addition the reference to 'animism' seems extremely unsatisfactory. Animism, as commonly understood, is the view, often attributed to primitive man, that certain events in nature, such as the movement of clouds or the occurrence of fire or lightning, are the result of personal activity. 'If the wind blows', says Gilbert Murray (1935, p. 23), 'it is because some being more or less human, though of course superhuman, is blowing with his cheeks.' This, however, is clearly a primitive view and cannot possibly have any claim to be 'intellectually respectable', while the allegedly rival view, 'Mind is a bodily process', is left completely unexplained. Moreover, if two views are 'intellectually respectable' one wonders how Hebb can justify his claim that modern psychologists are committed to only one of them. Again, when he says that 'there is . . . no decisive means available of proving one to be right, the other wrong', one suspects that he has not fully worked out what he is saying: to assert that an attempted proof was unsuccessful entails the existence of a criterion of success, and in this case it is hard to see how such a criterion could be formulated. In any situation where one is tempted to believe that 'no proof is possible' it is salutary to remember the dictum of Wittgenstein (1953, section 220), 'One can often say in mathematics: let the *proof* teach you *what* was being proved.' Finally, Hebb says that one can work with a theory 'on an "as-if" basis' without having to believe it. This is surely the height of paradox, and indeed it is hard to suppose that he is using the word 'believe' in its normal sense. Even the analogy with chemistry ('We study the mind in the same way as a chemist studies the atom') is more confusing than helpful: it is perfectly possible from observation of a person's behaviour to infer that certain events are going on inside his head, and if, hypothetically, his head were cut open and the events in it made available for inspection, no such inference would be needed. If the analogy is to hold, however, there would have to be some comparable situation in chemistry ('direct observation of the atom'), and this idea is problematic to say the least. Hebb's account implies that there are similarities where none exist.

We should like to conclude this section by suggesting that arguments about materialism, metaphysical behaviourism, and methodological behaviourism should now be laid to rest, since they are the products of conceptual confusion. The insights of the analytical behaviourist, in contrast, are an important contribution to conceptual analysis, and we shall be making further use of them in Chapter 6. As far as behaviourism in general is concerned, the word has by now acquired so many different strands of meaning that proclamations that one is 'for' or 'against' it are unlikely to serve any useful purpose.

3. *Cluster theory*

Ryle devotes the last chapter of *The Concept of Mind* to a discussion of how to characterize psychology. He writes as follows:

> The abandonment of the dream of psychology as a counterpart to Newtonian science, as this was piously misrepresented, involves abandonment of the notion that 'psychology' is the name of a unitary enquiry or tree of enquiries. Much as 'Medicine' is the name of a somewhat arbitrary consortium of more or less loosely connected enquiries and techniques, a consortium which neither has, nor needs, a logically trim statement of programme, so 'psychology' can quite conveniently be used to denote a partly fortuitous federation of inquiries and techniques . . . The recognition that there are many sciences should remove the sting from the suggestion that 'psychology' is not the name of a single homogeneous theory. Few of the names of sciences do denote such unitary theories, or show any promise of doing so. Nor is 'cards' the name either of a single game or of a 'tree' of games. (Ryle, 1949, pp. 323–324)

We shall refer to this view as a 'cluster' theory about the subject matter of psychology. Its essential feature is the thesis that there need be no one single line of enquiry which all psychologists ought to share, since in fact they pursue a variety (or 'cluster') of enquiries which may be interrelated in a variety of ways.

A similar view has recently been put forward by Beloff, who writes: 'As soon as one attempts to say what psychology is about, it becomes clear that one is dealing not with a single unified science, but with a collection of more or less loosely affiliated disciplines each with its own peculiar concepts and laws, its own methods and techniques' (Beloff, 1973, p. ix). Even more provocatively Koch writes: 'Students should no longer be tricked by a terminological rhetoric into the belief that they are studying a single discipline' (Koch, 1974, p. 26).

An area where cluster theory seemed particularly plausible was that of social psychology. Systematic observations of the behaviour of people in crowds was recognized as a possible line of research; and it was agreed that one might keep careful records of the behaviour of children in schools, patients in hospital, and offenders in prison or Borstal with a view to discovering what were the influences of social factors. It was possible, too, to give people attitude question-naires and to study in laboratory conditions the effect on the subjects' performance of the presence of an audience. In general, there was no dearth of empirical data but very little by way of systematic unified enquiry. There was, indeed, a story circulating in Oxford in the 1940's about a student who was taking a course in social psychology and who approached his tutor for advice on what books to read. The tutor's first response was, 'Whatever you do, don't read McDougall.' When asked, 'Then what *shall* I read?', however, the tutor paused and after considerable hesitation said, 'Perhaps you *had* better read McDougall!' Such, apparently, was the dearth of good books on social psychology at the time. Even the appearance of Sprott's classic work on the subject (Sprott, 1952) did little to suggest the existence of any unified subject matter. One of the present authors, reviewing this book in *Mind*, wrote:

> The shop labelled 'social psychology' sells a remarkable miscellany of goods: and, despite the excellence of Professor Sprott's stocktaking, it is questionable if all these goods should have gone into the same department ... There are psychologies labelled, for instance, 'general', 'social', 'experimental', 'educational', 'physiological' and 'child'; but they are certainly not mutually exclusive and they qualify the word 'psychology' in different ways. If social psychology is a single subject, the contributors to it are a curiously mixed bunch, and include, *inter alios*, Marx, Freud, Malinowski, Hitler, and Gallup. Such a classification cuts through the middle of perception, intelligence testing, and psychoanalysis, and unites the work of Burt and Isaacs with the Gallup poll. (Miles, 1954, p. 558)

A great merit of cluster theory is its recognition that the word 'psychology', like other words, is open-ended. It is unnecessary, in other words, to suppose that there is one single thing which psychology *is* (any more than there is a single thing which learning or intelligence *is*), and it is therefore perfectly possible for worthwhile enquires to be conducted without there being, in Ryle's words, any 'logically trim statement of programme'. As an account of the state of psychology when *The Concept of Mind* was first published in 1949, Ryle's formulation seems to us to be perfectly correct.

This does not, of course, mean that a single formula is ruled out in principle; and the search for unity among diversity has been an important characteristic in many areas of human thought. It remains, therefore, to discuss two recent attempts to 'unify' the subject matter of psychology, i.e. to draw boundaries in such a way that the result is an identifiable distinctive discipline. These two attempts are cybernetic theory and operant theory.

4. *Cybernetic theory*

The cybernetic approach owes its origin to the development by Shannon and Weaver (1949) of the mathematics of information theory. Psychologists were quick to see the possible applications of information theory to their own subject (see, for example, Broadbent, 1958; Attneave, 1959; Miller, Galanter, and Pribram, 1960; Brown, 1966), and many exciting ideas for experiment were generated.

The basic conceptual innovation here was the replacement of the word 'stimulus' by the word 'input'. The organism was treated as a transmitter of information, and experiments were conducted using the concepts of *redundancy, channel capacity, noise, feedback*, etc. The study of perception thus became the study of the organism's immediate output when particular inputs were supplied, and the study of memory became the study of output after controlled amounts of delay. In the latter case questions were also asked about the mechanisms by which the input was 'stored' inside the organism and made available for use as output. Psychology, on this showing, is the search for relationships between input and output and the attempt to understand the underlying mechanisms.

One of the exciting things about cybernetic theory, in contrast with cluster theory, is its comprehensiveness. As far as psychology is concerned, the cybernetic approach, if applicable at all, is applicable 'across the board'. In other words *any* investigation among those traditionally made by psychologists allows of redescription in these terms. Possibly in some cases the fit is not entirely comfortable, for instance if one describes a printed personality questionnaire as 'input' and the subject's written response to it as 'output'; from the nature of the case, however, such a redescription is logically possible.

In addition, the tiresome 'outsider', social psychology, can be fitted in. Sometimes, one may say, the input owes its origin not to an inanimate object but to a living organism, and social psychology is the study of outputs when at least some inputs are of this kind. There is, of course, no reason why a machine should not be programmed to take account of social factors.

Another exciting thing about cybernetic theory is that it combines the scientific rigour of a mechanistic approach with the reintroduction of mentalistic concepts. It was, of course, plain on empirical grounds that living organisms did not always respond consistently to what in physical terms was the same input, nor did different individuals, whether of the same or different species, necessarily respond alike. Previous experience was clearly relevant, as were the mechanisms, or potential mechanisms, with which the organism had been genetically endowed. Cybernetic theory, therefore, was not crudely 'mechanistic' in the sense of assuming that living organisms responded in stereotyped ways to a particular 'input' regardless of the context in which it was presented. Psychologists thus had a conceptual scheme which enabled them to take seriously the obvious fact that they themselves and their subjects—or at any rate their human subjects—could plan and could take account of possible situations as opposed to actual ones. It is not difficult to envisage a mechanism which 'searches' until if finds an input matching the one with which it has already been programmed, and this, if we speak mentalistically, is termed 'recognition'. Similarly one can think of a device as a result of which the effect of a particular contact (with, say, knob B as opposed to knob A) was fed back into a central mechanism, the latter having been programmed to search for or avoid such results; and in this case one could speak, in mentalistic terms, of 'weighing alternatives' or 'choosing'. One of the remarkable things about humans in particular, on this showing, is their ability to give the correct answer from a wide range of choices. If we consider the repertoire of sounds which are vocally possible for any human being, even a young child, it is perhaps right to feel a sense of wonder at the extent to which linguistic communication is possible. To use the mathematical terminology which became fashionable in the early days of information theory, a human being can transmit an extremely large number of 'bits' of information in a short time. In this respect he is different from a rat, whose information processing abilities are very much less.

On this view the difference between humans and so-called 'lower' organisms is preserved, but without any departure from the policy of looking for a mechanical explanation of their various skills. It seems to us likely that when George Miller (1966) entitled a popular book *Psychology: the Science of Mental Life* he was making a deliberate challenge to some of his more behaviouristically-minded colleagues.

The application to psychology of ideas originally used in communication engineering is not, of course, without difficulties. In particular, from the point of view of the telephone engineer humans are at the two ends, while the system whose efficiency is being studied is at the centre. In contrast psychology places the human 'recording instrument' at the centre with non-human instruments at each end whose function is to provide inputs and record outputs. Although this difference does not invalidate the use of cybernetic concepts in psychology, it can still be a source of conceptual confusion. This is because communication engineering presupposes a difference between recording instruments and listener, and if a psychologist then insists that the listener is *himself* a recording instrument he is using the words 'recording instrument' without a polar term. He might even be tempted to postulate some kind of ghostly listener to read off the answers from the (human) recording device whose properties he was studying, though this would not help him unless the ghostly listener was himself immune from being regarded as a communication channel!

We shall be returning to the cybernetic approach in Chapter 7. For the moment all that need be said is that in our view it is not fully satisfactory since it involves a basic ambiguity. Thus although it makes sense to ask what goes on inside the 'black box' between input and output, and to postulate appropriate 'models', the status of these models remains uncertain. One possibility is for psychologists to claim without qualification that they are investigating how the nervous system works. If this is so, however, such research should in our opinion more properly be classified as physiology and take place in a physiological context. If, on the other hand, the objective is thought to be postulation of some kind of purely theoretical explanatory fiction bearing no necessary resemblance to any actual nervous system, then such models are no more than devices for generating predictions as to further relationships between input and output; and in that case the emphasis has shifted from a cybernetic approach to an operant one. But whereas operant psychology does not profess to do anything other than study relationships between input and output, there is every temptation on the cybernetic formula to suppose that one is studying such things as storage and retrieval systems, the decay of traces, and the transmission of information.

These considerations do not, of course, imply that experiments with a cybernetic orientation are a waste of time. They do, however, suggest the possibility of a simplified redescription. Theoretical models may help in deciding what stimuli to present, but if one is studying what lawful relations exist between stimuli and responses it is misleading to imply that one is doing anything else.

5. Operant theory

Operant theory shares with cybernetic theory the view that psychology involves the study of the relationships between 'input' and 'output' (or 'stimulus' and 'response'), but its conceptual scheme has no place for statements purporting to be about the neural correlates of behaviour, such statements being regarded not, of course, as false but simply as irrelevant. Moreover it is like cybernetic theory in being applicable 'across the board': thus any situation which a psychologist chooses to study must as a matter of logic admit of being described in terms of behaviour-being-reinforced, and it must therefore necessarily make sense to ask what are the effects of varying the contingencies of reinforcement in certain ways. It is also like cybernetic theory in that it does not deny the existence or dispute the importance of so-called 'higher mental processes'. Thus, as will be seen more fully in Chaper 6, even in situations where the subject is required to do no more than press a lever, considerable mental prowess may still be needed if he is to press the right lever at the right time.

Finally, operant theory shares with analytical behaviourism the view that statements about a person's mental life, mental powers, etc., require to be translated into statements about his actual or possible behaviour. Whereas analytical behaviourism is content to describe psychology as 'the science of behaviour', however, an important characteristic of operant theory is its emphasis on the study of an individual over a period of time rather than in a once-and-for-all situation. Psychology on this showing is the study of the *interaction* between organism and environment: to put the matter in a somewhat provocative way, when an organism acts the environment *hits back*, and this in its turn influences what the organism does next. For an operant psychologist it is important that this interplay should be emphasized.

Our argument has been that discussions about the subject matter of psychology should be regarded as conceptual in character. A particular formula is therefore helpful in so far as it emphasizes appropriate similarities and differences, and is unhelpful in so far as it misclassifies by implying the existence of similarities, analogies, or parallels where none exist. In the last resort, therefore, the answer to the question 'What is the subject matter of psychology?' is 'Say what you like'. As we have seen, this does not mean that no one formula is better than any other; but it means that one is in a position to decide between formulae not in a spirit of dogmatism (in Kant's sense) but on the basis of what particular similarities and differences one wishes to emphasize.

To sum up, those who have done the appropriate conceptual analysis are perhaps unlikely to want to say that psychology is the study of mental occurrences as opposed to physical ones; this is not because there are no such occurrences (in the sense in which there are no such things as dragons), nor because such occurrences are unsuitable for scientific study, but because the assumption that all mentalistic words stand for occurrences is misguided. Nor, on the other hand, will they be content with the dictum that 'all that we can observe is behaviour', since this implies an analogy with situations where it makes sense to speak of the observation or discovery of something additional. In contrast, they will recognize that sentences containing mentalistic words can in many contexts be translated into sentences about behaviour and that within psychology there may be different questions which are not necessarily all capable of solution by the same methods or techniques. Whether they choose to substitute the words 'input' and 'output' for the words 'stimulus' and 'response' will depend on the value which they place on the implied analogies; and if, like the present authors, they prefer the operant to the cybernetic approach they will say that psychology is *the study of the interaction between organism and environment*. It is unhelpful, however, merely to *assert* this formula; to demonstrate its value it is necessary to show what can be achieved by means of it.

In saying that disagreements about the subject matter of psychology are conceptual in character we are not, of course, implying that conceptual analysis will cause all such disagreements to disappear, since it may indeed be an inescapable fact that different psychologists wish to emphasize different procedures and classifications. One cannot carry out conceptual analysis effectively, however, without knowing the rules of the 'language-game' which is being played, or, in other words, without understanding why an apparent 'opponent' wishes to order his concepts as he does. To treat an issue as conceptual in character must therefore lead to greater understanding; and indeed it is impossible as a matter of logic to disagree with a conceptual proposal unless one has fully understood all the reasons for making it. In our view psychology is not torn with disagreement to anywhere near the extent which some people have supposed; in so far, however, as such disagreement does exist it can helpfully be viewed as disagreement over choice of concepts, in which case one needs to bear in mind that different emphases may be helpful for different purposes.

Chapter 5

Operant Psychology as an Example of Conceptual Revision

A distinction was drawn in Chapter 2 between statements about how particular concepts function ('conceptual analysis') and proposals for innovation ('conceptual revision'). In this chapter we shall suggest that operant psychology can be regarded as a series of proposals for conceptual revision.

Our claim is not, of course, that statements which use the idioms of ordinary language are always false, but rather that for special experimental purposes a different set of concepts is needed. For example, although the concepts *learn, remember, recognize*, and *know* are serviceable for many purposes, if we require a systematic record of what happened in a particular situation they may not be precise enough; and it is therefore necessary instead to record what the subject did in response to particular stimuli and to note what stimuli make a particular class of responses more probable.

As well as the basic concepts of *reinforcer* and *discriminative stimulus* (S^D) operant psychologists have also required concepts for describing ways in which stimuli can be planned by the experimenter so as to be contingent upon particular responses by the subject; these are the various *schedules of reinforcement*. Similarly it may be necessary to refer to the absence of a particular discriminative stimulus (S^Δ) or to the absence for a given time of any change in stimulation (*time out*). There are also concepts connected with the subject's responses and their description, in particular *response rate, baseline, steady state, interresponse time,* and *post-reinforcement pause*. Finally, as we shall see more fully in Chapter 6, there are the concepts which operant psychology shares with most scientific approaches: stimuli and responses can be described in terms of their position in space, their position in time, their number, and their intensity.

It is perhaps helpful to say that what is being recommended in operant psychology is a 'programme of translation', in the sense given to these words on p. 17. Psychologists are being invited to redescribe familiar situations using the technical terms given above. Any situation can on this showing be seen as a case of behaviour-being-reinforced; and the central thesis is that the question 'What kinds of stimulus will make this or that behaviour more frequent?' is a helpful one to ask.

The following passage from Skinner indicates very clearly the kind of 'translation' which we have in mind:

Consider a young man whose world has suddenly changed. He has graduated from college and is going to work, let us say, or has been inducted into the armed services. Most of the behaviour he has acquired up to this point proves useless in his new environment. The behaviour he actually exhibits can be described, and the description translated, as follows: he lacks assurance or feels insecure or is unsure of himself (*his behaviour is weak and inappropriate*); he is dissatisfied or discouraged (*he is seldom reinforced, and as a result his behaviour undergoes extinction*); he is frustrated (*extinction is accompanied by emotional responses*): he feels uneasy or anxious (*his behaviour frequently has unavoidable aversive consequences which have emotional effects*); there is nothing he wants to do or enjoys doing well, he has no feeling of craftsmanship, no sense of leading a purposeful life, no sense of accomplishment (*he is rarely reinforced for doing anything*); he feels guilty or ashamed (*he has previously been punished for idleness or failure, which now evokes emotional responses*); he is disappointed in himself or disgusted with himself (*he is no longer reinforced by the admiration of others, and the extinction which follows has emotional effects*); he becomes hypochondriacal (*he concludes that he is ill*) or neurotic (*he engages in a variety of ineffective modes of escape*); and he experiences an identity crisis (*he does not recognize the person he once called 'I'*).

The italicized paraphrases are too brief to be precise, but they suggest the possibility of an alternative account, which alone suggests effective action. To the young man himself the important things are no doubt the various states of his body. They are salient stimuli, and he has learned to use them in traditional ways to explain his behaviour to himself and others. What he tells us about his feelings may permit us to make some informed guesses about what is wrong with the contingencies, but we must go directly to the contingencies if we want to be sure, *and it is the contingencies which must be changed if his behaviour is to be changed.* (Skinner, 1972, pp. 146–147)

As Skinner would doubtless agree, his translation as it stands has much of the inexactness of the original formulation. It is mistaken, however, to object that it merely says the same thing in a less elegant jargon. On the contrary, it points to possible action, since it invites both the person himself and others to consider what stimuli are most likely to reinforce, i.e. make more frequent, whatever behaviour is selected for study. It might still be objected that, even if Skinner has shown 'in principle' how such a translation might be made, he would still be in considerable difficulty if pressed to support his proposals in detail. This, however, is a misunderstanding (possibly arising from the extension in meaning of the word 'translation', see p. 17). It is not that Skinner might have given a more accurate translation if he had taken more time and trouble (as would be the case, for instance, if someone were attempting to translate Virgil from Latin into English and failed to bring out some of the subtle nuances). His reformulation should be regarded simply as a reminder of how particular situations can be reappraised as cases of 'behaviour-being-reinforced'. Greater precision can come only when one records in detail what were the relevant stimuli to which the subject was exposed and what he did in response to them. Similarly the value of the operant programme of translation is not contingent upon the truth of particular empirical claims. It may or may not be true that if a child is given sweets there is an increase in the number of appropriate responses which he emits. In point of fact there is evidence (Harzem, 1975; Harzem and Damon, 1976) that different children are reinforced by different things—an obvious truth, perhaps, which surprisingly has often been overlooked. In the long run, of course, empirical findings can legitimately lead a research worker to modify—or even to abandon—the conceptual scheme which he was using; for example, if persistence with the question 'What is reinforcing?' were found after several decades to have yielded only trivial results, this would provide logical justification for no longer using the concept of a *reinforcer*. In the short run, however, the conceptual claim that 'What is reinforcing?' is a good question to ask does not commit the speaker to any particular empirical claim as to what in a given set of circumstances *is* reinforcing.

What is being offered is in effect a conceptual scheme which encourages people to view many facets of human and animal behaviour in a new way. In our present society it may well be—either through absence of planning or because the planning is inefficient—that the wrong kinds of behaviour are reinforced. This point can be illustrated by a series of examples. Although we may not know for certain what stimuli will be reinforcing in a particular case, it is possible to make informed judgements of what is likely; and on the basis of such judgements one may question the wisdom of particular policies. (There is, of course, an extra complication if there is disagreement as to what objectives are desirable, but this is a separate issue to which we shall be returning in Chapter 8.) As things are, for instance, the actions which we call 'going on strike' are frequently followed by an increase in pay; and since such an increase is likely to have a reinforcing effect, the operant approach forces one to ask whether more could be done to reward those who do *not* resort to such coercion. It would be interesting, too, to apply operant principles to the study of car drivers. As Cherry (1962, pp. 186–187) has interestingly pointed out, the amount of information which can pass between one car and another is very limited: indeed there is little that a driver can do other than flash his lights, sound his horn, and signal acknowledgement; and one wonders if more steps could be taken to ensure that there was suitable reinforcement for appropriate behaviour on the roads. Insurance companies do, of course, give a financial bonus to those who make 'no claims', and this may well have a reinforcing effect on careful driving; and on operant principles it would be appropriate to introduce a system of taxation by which those with an accident-free record paid less. Similarly, when decisions are involved about handling of children, parents and teachers may well find it helpful to ask themselves whether a particular action on their own part is likely to have a reinforcing effect or the opposite. In some cases, as many of them well know, a child who displays unwanted behaviour—a temper tantrum for instance—is best left alone, since (in operant terminology) the stimuli which occur when someone pays attention to such behaviour may well have a reinforcing effect. Again if one wishes pupils in a class to contribute to discussion it is clearly wise policy to praise their efforts where possible rather than offer carping criticisms. It is also worth remembering that publicity—including unfavourable publicity—can sometimes have a reinforcing effect. Not long ago there was a controversy in the press as to whether someone who planned to make a film on the sex-life of Jesus Christ should be allowed into the country; those who wished to discourage such film making would surely have done better to ignore the proposed film rather than denounce it.

These examples show how any social situation can be viewed as a case of behaviour-being-reinforced. It follows that if one chooses to study such situations by means of systematic research one has a ready-made starting-point, that of considering what stimuli are most likely to be reinforcing. One will then need to ask what time intervals are needed between one stimulus and the next, or between a response and a stimulus which is contingent upon it, if particular patterns of responding are to be maintained or changed. The claim is not that operant psychology knows the answers to such questions in advance, but that the questions themselves are helpful ones to ask. In some cases there may even be laboratory research which has already reproduced the most important features of particular situations, e.g. those involving the use of punishment (cf. Chapter 11); and where this is the case research need not start *de novo*.

It is sometimes supposed that the fact that man is a language user is in some way a problem for the operant psychologist. When Skinner (1957) discusses this matter, however, it is clear that he is not disputing the obvious empirical truth that people can learn rules and produce original sentences; indeed he is not making any specific predictions at all. His purpose is rather to show that the same conceptual scheme which in his view had already proved effective in the study of other types of behaviour is applicable in the case of 'verbal behaviour' also. His intention is thus in effect to encourage psychologists to consider what are the variables which control such behaviour: in an educational setting, for example, they might choose to investigate a whole range of topics in connection with the acquisition of language skills, while in a clinical setting they might study the extent to which the verbal responses of aphasic and non-aphasic patients are under the control of different stimuli.

It is, of course, no part of the operant thesis to deny that the concept of *meaning* is important or to deny that sentences of the form 'X knows the meaning of . . .' are ever true. What is important in operant psychology is to arrive at a correct logical analysis (or 'translation') of such sentences and to avoid mystifying language about 'entities called meanings' such as sometimes occurs in the writings of the sophisticated. This is yet a further area where Wittgenstein's policy of 'bring[ing] words back from their metaphysical to their everyday usage' (cf. p. 21) is likely to pay dividends, As Austin (1961, pp.23 ff.) has pointed out, it makes sense to ask what is the meaning of a particular word, but general questions such as 'What is the-meaning-of-a-word?' (with hyphens) and 'What is the "meaning" of a word?' can be seen on inspection to be nonsense.

With regard to alleged disagreements on the subject of language between Skinner and Chomsky, these seem to us to be not so much disagreements as arguments at cross purposes. Skinner's thesis, as we have noted already, is that psychologists can profitably examine the variables which control human verbal behaviour, whereas Chomsky is concerned with several quite different problems, for example the question of what rules a speaker is implicitly following when he generates meaningful sentences. If X and Y are asking questions that are different in logical type, it is surely plain that there can be neither agreement nor disagreement between them.

Whether there exists some kind of 'innate language mechanism' is an empirical matter, and its truth or falsity is therefore irrelevant to the conceptual proposals which are central to operant psychology. Indeed, those who assume that Chomsky and his followers are or could be in a position, on the basis of *evidence*, to 'refute Skinner's theory of language acquisition' have missed the point of what Skinner is trying to say. The following passage, for example, typifies what we believe to be a widespread misunderstanding:

> Skinner . . . argues that verbal behaviour, being no different from all other behaviour, is fully explicable as the result of specific stimulus–response reinforcement contingencies . . . Other psychologists have argued that it is impossible to explain people's language behaviour, particularly the ability to produce novel meaningful sentences, without allowing for knowledge of meanings and of the rules for expressing them linguistically. (Greene, 1975, pp.82–83)

It is, of course, possible to ask, in connection with human verbal behaviour, questions other than 'What are the controlling variables?', but if these are what one has chosen to study, it makes no sense to discuss whether or not human verbal behaviour is 'fully explicable' within this framework; and even if the isolation of controlling variables in a particular area turned out to be difficult, one would still not be justified in postulating the existence of entities other than controlling variables as if this solved the difficulty! Such entities would at best be indicators of what is not yet known.

Moreover, since operant psychology (at least in our version of it) is not committed to *particular* empirical claims of any kind but only to a specified conceptual scheme, there is no logical need for an operant psychologist, *qua* operant psychologist, to make any distinctive claims about the relative influences of 'nature' and 'nurture'. There is no reason why the many components of what is loosely called 'genetic make-up' should not function as controlling variables, and indeed it is plain that they do so: some of the verbal responses of a colour-blind person, for instance, are under different stimulus control from those of a person who is not colour-blind. How large is the influence of such factors, or, conversely, how far behaviour can be brought under the control of present influences is an empirical question; and the conceptual stipulation 'Ask what are the controlling variables' does not entail the falsity of any empirical claim about the relative influences of 'nature' and 'nurture'.

It has also been supposed that in two major areas of recent research there is evidence which contradicts or undermines the claims of operant psychology. One such piece of evidence is the discovery that operant and respondent types of behaviour may be similar in more respects than was previously supposed. In particular many autonomic responses, such as heart rate, contraction of blood vessels, and the like, may be affected by their consequences as an operant response is affected by its consequence. Conversely, too, it has been suggested that some operant responses, notably the pigeon's key-pecks, can be *elicited* by stimuli preceding them in the same way as respondents are elicited. Second, there are the phenomena which have been considered under the title 'constraints on learning': in particular it has been found that some behaviour patterns of animals are less amenable to modification by reinforcement than are others. These two areas have attracted so much attention in recent years that it might be wondered why we have not devoted more of these pages to discussing them. Both issues, however, are empirical. The fact that some elicited responses are controlled, like operant responses, by their consequences cannot as a matter of logic undermine the conceptual foundations of operant psychology; and the fact that some responses are less amenable to reinforcement than others cannot detract from the importance of the question, 'What is reinforcing?' In the long run concepts which turn out to be unhelpful should of course be abandoned; but those who claim that these experimental findings constitute on their own a 'refutation of operant psychology' have failed to draw the distinction between conceptual issues and empirical ones.

Operant psychology, then, involves a programme of conceptual revision. In this connection some interesting parallels suggest themselves with the work of Ryle (1949). It would be fair to say that Ryle was concerned to analyse concepts rather than revise them; and it was no part of his programme to try to change the language habits of 'teachers and examiners, magistrates and critics, confessors and non-commissioned officers, employers, employees and partners, parents, lovers, friends, and enemies' (Ryle, 1949, p.7). By calling attention, however, to the classifications implicit in the mentalistic concepts which ordinary people use for workaday purposes, he was able to exhibit the *mis*classifications perpetrated by philosophers.

Skinner, in contrast, has been concerned to change such language—not, indeed, on the grounds that it is inadequate for ordinary communication but because it is inadequate in a science of behaviour. 'English', he says (Skinner, 1972, p.23), 'is full of prescientific terms which usually suffice for purposes of casual discourse. No one looks askance at the astronomer when he says that the sun rises or that the stars come out at night.' For research purposes, however, such language lacks precision and gives no clear guide as to how people's behaviour can be changed. Psychologists may well *start* their research under the influence of familiar mentalistic concepts: they may claim, for instance, that they wish to study learning or memory or intelligence or motivation, but as soon as they attempt to keep a detailed record of what happened they are likely to find such terms inadequate.

It is plain on examination, however, that Ryle's programme of analysing our concepts and Skinner's programme of revising them have much in common. Thus neither Ryle nor Skinner is committed to denying that sentences such as 'He has an alert mind' are sometimes true, and both are interested in the question of what has to happen to make them true. Moreover both implicitly recognize (though they might not say this in as many words) that the contrast between 'mental' and 'physical' happenings is at least problematic and perhaps illegitimate. Thus Skinner (1953, p.282) points out the absurdity of accepting this conjunction and then saying that some events, viz. mental ones, are not suitable objects for scientific study. Similarly Ryle (1949), through skilful use of the *reductio ad absurdum* argument, exhibits how unnecessary and misleading it is for philosophers to think of 'kinds of event' or 'kinds of entity' in this way. The following is a characteristic quotation from a later work:

> A soldier obeys the order to halt. The behaviourist witnesses just the One bodily act of halting, with no obeying; the Cartesian adds one piece of obeying to one act of halting and gets Two . . .—well! Two *whats*? . . . Cross-category counting yields neither a couple nor a singleton of 'them', where there can be no 'they'. (Ryle, 1974, p.7)

Ryle and Skinner would agree further that there is no one single event which would provide definitive justification for asserting that someone has an alert mind. Many words which ascribe qualities of intellect and character to people are—to use Ryle's phrase—'dispositional' in character: they indicate how the person is disposed to behave on a variety of occasions. For many purposes this 'openness' of ordinary speech to which Ryle has directed our attention is an advantage; we can indicate the *kinds* of things which a person often does without having to specify them to the last detail, much as we can use words such as 'a few' or 'several' without having to specify exactly how many. In a science of behaviour, however, one needs a full specification of what exactly the subject said or did in response to what. Thus it may be perfectly adequate for workaday purposes to say that a child 'knows his six times table'; this tells us what he would do, or is capable of doing, on a variety of occasions. For experimental purposes, however, it may be important to record, for instance, whether he was simply asked, 'Recite your six times table', whether he was required to put in the preliminary phrases such as 'One six is . . .', 'Two sixes are . . .' (since this has been found to make a difference; see Miles and Wheeler, 1974), or whether he was asked specific questions such as, 'What is six times nine?' For experimental purposes, therefore, the word 'know' requires to be 'translated out'.

It has often been supposed, not least by the present authors, that this programme of translation encounters a difficulty whenever there is a reference to so-called 'private' events, e.g. dreams, toothaches, or mental images. Thus 'X has toothache' is plainly not equivalent to 'X is wincing', 'X is holding his jaw', 'X is saying, "ouch!"', 'X is announcing, "I have toothache"', or any combination of such statements. Similarly people can *report* on their dreams or on their mental images but this, it is said, is not the same as *having* them. Even more problematic, it seems, are first-person sentences such as 'I have toothache', since there are clearly occasions when I am entitled to say this without first having to discover myself wincing or ringing up the dentist!

This problem was comprehensively discussed by Wisdom (1952), and relatively little need be added here. It is an obvious empirical truth that one may sometimes be unsure whether someone has toothache or is reporting his dream correctly, and although it is easy to recognize how such a thesis arises, it is none the less a curious conceptual innovation to suggest that we can *never* be sure of such matters. There are, of course, some situations involving use of the first person where the question of sureness or its opposite does not arise; for example, it is difficult to see what uses there could be for the expression 'I am unsure whether I am in pain' (cf. Wittgenstein, 1953, section 408). The basic problem, however, at least in the case of third-person statements, seems to be that of pointing to a paradigm case—something that would count as a definitive observation—since otherwise how could the meaning of words such as 'toothache' ever have been learned? 'X knows his six times table' can be 'unpacked' definitively; to know one's six times table just *is* to be able to respond in certain ways, and if a child is to learn how to use the word 'know' it is logically necessary that he should be exposed to definitive cases of this sort. But what situation would definitively justify the use of the words 'X has toothache'? Yet if it is said that we infer the toothache—a 'private' event—from the occurrence of 'public' events such as wincing, it is impossible as a matter of logic that any of us could ever have learned what the word 'toothache' meant.

Skinner has pointed out (1953, pp.257–258) that part of our environment is enclosed within our own skin. 'A private event may be distinguished by its limited accessibility but not, so far as we know, by any special structure or nature. We have no reason to suppose that the stimulating effect of an inflamed tooth is essentially different from that of, say, a hot stove.' If this is correct, as we believe it is, then the definitive occurrence in the case of so-called 'private' events lies in the experience of one particular individual; it is an empirical fact that in the case of others no such definitive occurrences are available (unless indeed one considers the possibility, for example, of 'wiring up' X's inflamed tooth to the appropriate part of Y's brain). This does not prevent the child from learning the meaning of words such as 'toothache' or 'dream'. As with all words one must assume that in the first place he hears adults saying them and later attempts to say them himself. If he uses them wrongly, e.g. by saying 'Did you notice my dream?', corrective stimuli will then come from the adults, and in due course he may find that if he talks about stoves the adults will say such things as 'Yes, I can see it, too', whereas if he talks about his toothache, dreams, or mental images their reactions are different. The fact that the child can learn to use these words correctly is no more and no less puzzling than, for instance, his ability to learn the use of personal pronouns.

Postscript

From what has been said both in Chapter 1 and in the present chapter the extent of our debt to Skinner will have become plain. At this stage of the book, however, it may be helpful if we try to summarize the main points where we have followed his lead without reservation and also indicate some further points where we believe him to have fallen into error. We embark on the latter task not in order to 'win' some kind of argument but simply in order to rid operant psychology of various accretions which are unnecessary and which may divert attention from its major insights.

Among the points of agreement we should like to mention the following in particular. (a) The basic suggestion that psychologists should study the *interaction* between organism and environment seems to us crucial. (b) As a matter of logic, we agree that it is unneccessary in such a study to use either physiological concepts or mentalistic ones. Both sets of concepts involve 'appeals to events taking place somewhere else, at some other level of observation, described in different terms' (Skinner, 1950, p.193), and we accept his view that it is possible to do without them. (c) It seems to us a particularly exciting innovation to have pointed out that situations involving social inter-action can be regarded as cases of behaviour-being-reinforced. (d) To treat situations in this way is not to belittle man's achievements in art, literature, and religion, but 'what changes is the possibility of doing something' (Skinner, 1972, p.213). (e) He recognizes that what he is offering is in effect a programme of translation (Skinner, 1972, pp.146–147), and that 'no theory changes what it is a theory about' (1972, p.215). (f) He does not dispute that sentences containing mentalistic concepts can sometimes be true. For example, it would be entirely incorrect to accuse him of ignoring the concept of *consciousness*. 'Rather than ignore consciousness', he writes (1972, pp.190–191), 'an experimental analysis of behaviour has stressed certain crucial issues. The question is not whether a man can know himself but what he knows when he does so.'

In general our experience is that the more carefully one reads Skinner's writings the less justified one regards the strictures of those critics who misinterpret him and then say how mistaken he is!

The following are our criticisms. (a) As will be explained more fully in Chapter 10, we believe that he has misled himself over the concepts of *freedom* and *control*, and that the discussions about 'autonomous man' (Skinner, 1972, *passim*) are misguided and unnecessary (though this is not to say that useful conceptual insights could not be found if some of the things which he says were reformulated). (b) He occasionally appears to be making the logical error of using conceptual arguments to draw empirical conclusions. For example (1972, pp.20–21), he rebukes the Freudians for telling their patients that they are 'the architects of their own destinies', and implies that it is always false to say of a person's behaviour that it is 'his own achievement' (1972, p.101). These and similar confusions arise from his failure to look at expressions such as 'architect of his own destiny', 'own achievement', etc., in the language-game which is their original home. He fails to ask, in other words, what distinctions were originally being drawn. In point of fact the distinctions in question could quite well survive in the language-game which he himself is commending. Phrases such as 'own achievement' and 'architect of his own destiny' can be interpreted without serious discomfort in terms of the action of prior stimuli; thus one would say that a picture was someone's own achievement if no one else painted it, and one would say that a person was the architect of his own destiny in the absence of certain kinds of coercive stimuli emanating from other human agents. Similarly, when Skinner says, 'A person does not support a religion because he is devout; he supports it because of the contingencies arranged by the religious agency' (1972, p.116), this sounds like an empirical claim that devoutness is never *in fact* a motive; and this logically implies that people support religion from *other* motives, e.g. desire for esteem. Devoutness, however, and the contingencies arranged by the religious agency are not (as he implies) alternative explanations belonging to the same logical type; his point would have been better expressed if he had made clear that he was commending a certain *class* of explanations, viz. those which explain in terms of antecedent contingencies. It follows, of course, not that people never act from motives of devoutness, but that 'because'-statements which refer to motives (of which 'because he is devout' is an example) are in need of translation. As a matter of logic nothing empirical about particular people's motives can follow from this conceptual point; to suppose otherwise would be like trying to produce empirical rabbits from a conceptual hat. (c) The reference in Skinner (1969, pp.233 ff.) 'The Behaviour of Seeing' is logically confused. Having appreciated, quite correctly, that if a speaker is to have grounds for saying that X *saw* Y there must be something in the situation to provide such justification (otherwise no one could ever have learned the meaning of the word 'see'). Skinner writes as though this 'something' was a piece of behaviour called 'seeing'. The considerations adduced by Ryle demonstrate that the logic of the word 'see' is not of this kind.

> Special cognitive acts and operations have been postulated to answer to such verbs as 'see', 'hear', 'taste', 'deduce', and 'recall' in the way in which familiar acts and operations do answer to such verbs as 'kick', 'run', 'look', 'listen', 'wrangle', and 'tell'; as if to describe a person as looking and seeing were like describing him as walking and humming instead of being like describing him as angling and catching or searching and finding. (Ryle, 1949, p.151)

Skinner agrees with Ryle in not wishing to speak of 'cognitive acts' but he is mistaken in supposing that seeing must therefore be a behavioural act. (d) He makes the mistake of supposing that expressions such as 'disturbed personality' and 'feels jubilant' refer to 'indwelling agents' (Skinner, 1972, p.8)—a mistake which could have been avoided if he had understood the arguments of Ryle. (e) There are examples of unsatisfactory scholarship. For example, it seems very naïve to say (Skinner, 1972, p.11) that the Greek words *ate* and *menos* refer to 'non-physical things' without considering whether the Greeks of the classical period even possessed a word which could be translated as 'non-physical'. Similarly he seems quite prepared to say that 'value judgements' raise questions 'not about facts but about how people feel about facts' (1972, p.102) without apparently realizing that this view involves an account of ethical terms which has long been discredited (cf. Ayer, 1936, p.104). (f) His bold suggestion that operant psychology can supply a rational basis for ethics, as implied by the claim 'The only good things are positive reinforcers' (Skinner, 1972, p.107), seems to us highly questionable and is certainly not supported by any convincing arguments. (g) He appears to be confused over the concepts of *praise* and *blame*. Taking as his examples the television speaker who 'uses a prompter which is out of sight' and the lecturer who 'glances only surreptitiously at his notes' (Skinner, 1972, p.49) he points out that our admiration becomes less when we discover what was in fact happening. This example, however, cannot do the job which he requires it to do. In such a situation we were *mistaken* (as we afterwards realize) in supposing that there was spontaneity; it does not follow that we would have been wrong to admire the speaker if *in fact* his talk had been spontaneous. Skinner seems to be suggesting that any situation studied in a science of behaviour must necessarily be of the former kind—that because we can always ask, 'What were the controlling variables?', and can sometimes discover them even in the most unlikely cases, admiration is increasingly out of place. Certainly his examples establish that there are *some* situations where knowledge of the controlling variables affects whether or not we admire an action, but it does nothing to establish that this is true invariably. Indeed, if in this particular case we had learned that there was no hidden prompter or no surreptitious glancing at notes and that the speaker had displayed his skill as a result of years of dedicated practice, this new knowledge would make us more, not less, inclined to admire him. As we shall see in Chapter 10, what is predictable does not necessarily cease to be admirable.

A final point of disagreement deserves brief mention. Skinner, writing in a more imaginative vein, seems to believe that if operant principles were suitably applied on a wide enough scale then, in theory at least, this could lead to an ideal society or Utopia. Such, at any rate, seems to be the message of *Walden Two* (Skinner, 1962). There are empirical grounds, however, for questioning whether he is right. He appears to have overlooked the fact that it is often *rare* objects which reinforce. W. S. Gilbert, in *The Gondoliers*, tells of a country where

> Lord Chancellors were cheap as sprats
> And Bishops in their shovel hats
> Were plentiful as tabby cats.

The disadvantage, however, is that

> When ev'ry blessed thing you hold
> Is made of silver or of gold
> You long for simple pewter.

If one could draw up an inventory of 'things which reinforce' then it would theoretically be possible to create such things in sufficiently large numbers to ensure that appropriate behaviour was reinforced whenever it occurred. A stimulus, however, can be reinforcing in one context and not in another; and if particular stimuli became very frequent it is likely on empirical grounds that they would cease to reinforce. In brief, it is hard to see how adequate reinforcement would be possible unless certain things had a rarity value, yet if there were insufficient of these things to go round this would be incompatible with the concept of *Utopia*. We suggest, therefore, that claims about the possibility of using operant techniques in bringing about a 'perfect' or Utopian state of affairs should be viewed with caution.

These points of disagreement, however, do not seem to us to be of major importance; and we mention them simply in the hope of ensuring that the genuine insights of operant psychology are distinguished from incidental accretions.

Chapter 6

A Language without Extra-Episodic Words

We suggested in Chapter 4 that the word 'behaviourism' had acquired so many different strands of meaning that it was now no longer profitable to proclaim oneself to be either 'for' or 'against' it. We did, however, indicate our broad agreement with one particular thesis associated with behaviourism, viz. the proposal that for certain research purposes statements containing so-called 'mentalistic' words require translation. This, of course, is a conceptual matter, not an empirical claim about whether people ever feel toothache or dream dreams (which they do), nor a piece of advice to research workers encouraging them to study behaviour rather than study something else unspecified.

In this chapter we shall examine this conceptual claim in more detail. We shall try to show that, implicit in the operant programme, is the ideal of a language without extra-episodic words. The characterization of such a language seems to us to be of considerable theoretical interest since one can then exhibit by contrast some of the features which we take for granted in ordinary language, most of whose words are 'extra-episodic'. Perhaps more important, one can show that the behaviourist programme of translating sentences containing mentalistic words is a special case of a more general programme: such translation is needed not because of some unexplained objection to mentalistic words as such but because of a perfectly valid objection—for research purposes—to extra-episodic words.

We begin with an explanation of our use of the expression 'extra-episodic'. If someone says, 'X is walking down the road' his words refer to a single episode. The word 'walk' describes an activity and the total situation is one which could be photographed by a cine camera. Similarly the sentence 'X coughed' again relates to a single episode, and the cough could be recorded on a tape-recorder. In contrast, if during a game of bridge 'X revoked' is to be true, this entails that certain things were the case over and above the playing of a particular card by X. He would need to have put a card on the table in a particular context—a spade, for instance, even though hearts had been led and there was a heart in his hand—and to have made it reach the table in such a way that he was seen to be 'playing' the card, not letting it drop accidentally from his hand. (To raise one's arm at an auction sale is not necessarily to bid, though it can be unfortunate if the auctioneer understands it as such.) 'Revoke', then, in our terminology, is an 'extra-episodic' word, in contrast with 'walk' and 'cough' which are not. The distinction depends on the extent to which references to events *outside* a particular here-and-now occurrence are involved.

It would, of course, be perfectly possible to photograph X in the act of revoking, for example by placing the camera so that it recorded X's hand in process of playing, say, the two of spades. But if one looks up the word 'revoke' in the dictionary there will be no reference to the two of spades, nor are all instances of playing the two of spades necessarily revoking. Whether a particular word is correctly used often depends not only on the occurrence of a particular episode but on the context in which that episode occurs.

In an interesting passage Ryle (1949, p.142) raises the question of what is the difference between saying of a bird that it is flying south and saying that it is migrating. A possible answer is that flying south is a case of migrating if and only if it occurs in a particular context—at a particular time of year, for instance, and in accordance with known biological principles. Applying our proposed terminology one might say that 'is migrating' is an extra-episodic expression whereas 'is flying south' relates simply to one particular episode.

We had originally planned to speak of 'a language without disposition words' (see Ryle, 1949, Chapter 5; cf. p.55 of this book). When, however, we came to consider some of the words whose logical behaviour we wished to examine, we found that some of them were not dispositional at all. This is true, for example, of the word 'revoke'. We therefore settled for the somewhat ugly expression 'extra-episodic words' in order to highlight the ways in which use of particular expressions can involve commitment to belief in events occurring outside the particular episode under observation. It is possible that we may have taken some liberties with the word 'episode' here, but the distinction in logical behaviour between *walk* and *cough* on the one hand and *revoke* on the other is the main point of importance.

Another distinction needed in this chapter is that between words which relate to *specific* activities and words which, while excluding some possibilities, do not provide the same amount of detail. To adapt another example of Ryle's, it is impossible as a matter of logic for someone to prune his roses without gardening. 'X is gardening', we suggest, is neither dispositional, like 'X is a gardener', nor is it extra-episodic, since nothing outside the particular episode of, say, pruning roses is involved. It is, however, *non-specific*. It does not tell us, for example, whether in fact X is pruning his roses, weeding, or planting spring bulbs. If he is gardening he must be doing one out of a fairly restricted number of such things, but there is no indication which one it is.

A language which is fully specific and contains no extra-episodic words should perhaps be regarded as some kind of ideal limit, since there may not in practice by any form of words which relates solely to the here-and-now and gives every possible detail. Even 'X walked' does not tell us precisely what bodily movements were involved, while 'X coughed' does not tell us if the noise which he made was 'ahem' or something different, while the very act of naming a person or object presupposes belief in a degree of permanence and regularity which could in principle turn out to be mistaken. This point, however, does not affect our central thesis. It is still the case that certain words entail extra-episodic commitment more than others. It is therefore quite legitimate, for research purposes, to aim at a language which makes such commitment minimal, without being drawn into argument as to whether there could ever be no commitment at all.

Now it has in fact been an implicit part of the operant programme to describe results in precisely this way. Thus the expression 'X pressed the lever' records a single episode and tells us little else. In contrast, many of the 'mentalistic' words which figure in traditional philosophical and psychological discussion are extra-episodic in character. Our next task is therefore to look further at the logical behaviour of some of these words in order to compare them with the word 'press'. For illustration purposes we have selected four such words, viz. 'know', 'recognize', 'learn', and 'forget'.

The word 'know' does not directly specify any kind of episode at all. It makes no logical sense to speak of doing or failing to do some knowing, nor can one ask if such knowing was done carefully, reluctantly, etc. If we consider actual uses, for instance 'X knows his six times table', it is plain that this expression relates to a whole range of things which in appropriate circumstances X might be able to do. Indeed, if he were asked 'What is six times three?' and answered 'Eighteen', this would not on its own give definitive justification for asserting that he knew his six times table. The use of this expression commits the speaker to a set of additional statements—statements about what X could have done or would have done if the occasion demanded, for example correcting someone who said that six times three was twenty-four.

Similarly if X were to meet one of the authors of this book on the stairs and were to say, 'Hello, Miles!', this would normally be taken as logically sufficient grounds for saying 'X recognized Miles when he saw him'. Implicit, however, in use of the word 'recognize' is a claim about what X could have done or would have done if the circumstances had been different. If a parrot said 'Hello, Miles!' on such an occasion, the knowledge that it was a parrot is logically relevant to the way in which one would describe the situation. From this episode alone it would not be justifiable to say that the parrot *recognized* Miles; one would rather say, 'What an odd coincidence that it should say "Hello, Miles!" just at the right time!' This interpretation would be confirmed if Harzem then came up the stairs and the parrot again said, 'Hello, Miles!' Moreover, if the parrot regularly said 'Hello, Harzem!' and 'Hello, Miles!' on the correct occasions, our well-established knowledge of what parrots can and cannot do would lead us to suspect some trick, just as it was in fact ultimately found to be a trick when the horse, Clever Hans, tapped his hoof the appropriate number of times when asked, for example, to change vulgar fractions into decimals (see Katz, 1937). (He had in fact learned to stop tapping when members of his audience made small movements after the correct number of taps had been reached.) As a point of logic, however, if the parrot was consistently able to say 'Hello, Miles!' and 'Hello, Harzem!' in the correct context, then it is hard to see how one could avoid claiming that the parrot correctly recognized both of us. Whether parrots are ever able to do such things is, of course, an empirical matter; logically, however, it remains true that this would be a correct use of 'recognize' if they did.

The word 'learn', too, is extra-episodic in most of its uses. Thus to say that X has learned something entails that in a particular context he is displaying behaviour which he did not display at an earlier date, and without some reference to what happened earlier the word 'learn', at least in its ordinary sense, would be out of place. It is, of course, possible to photograph someone in the *process* of learning, for instance if he were learning his part in a play; but there is no one class of actions which such a photograph would consistently reveal, since the person might be pacing the room, sitting in a chair staring at the text, muttering to himself, and so on, and in a different context some of these activities might not count as 'learning'. Indeed, as was pointed out in Chapter 3, it is likely that there is no one single characteristic shared by all situations where the word 'learn' is correctly used, and even if such a characteristic were discovered it is not clear that this would necessarily constitute any major scientific advance. The word 'learn', like many others, has, in Wittgenstein's phrase (1953, section 77), a 'family of meanings', and to search, as psychologists of an earlier generation appear to have done, for the one and only correct 'theory of learning' was surely to indulge in a wild-goose chase. The wild goose, we are told, is very difficult to catch and is not much use when caught.

Finally, we should like to offer some comments on the logic of the word 'forget'. If 'X forgot to post the letter' is to be true, then clearly there must have been an episode of some kind, even if the word 'forget' does not itself refer to an identifiable class of occurrence which, like walking, has approximately the same properties on different occasions. For example, one can imagine a film, perhaps based on a Hardy-type novel, in which everything hinged on someone's not forgetting to post a letter: he might be shown, for instance, walking past a pillar box with the letter sticking out of his pocket, and talking, perhaps with his head in the air, about some subject quite remote from letter posting. Such behaviour, however, is not itself forgetting; there are other ways of forgetting than walking past a pillar box with one's head in the air, and not all such walking, if the context is different, is necessarily forgetting. Sentences containing the word 'forget' are in some ways like negative sentences; and just as one sometimes feels philosophical bewilderment if one tries to look for the episodes named by a person's *not* having done something, so one may be tempted to look for an episode which constitutes forgetting and then be puzzled because forgetting in another context involves a quite different set of episodes. The main source of the bewilderment is the assumption that all verbs are 'episodic' in character, and once this assumption is questioned there is no longer any need to feel puzzled. Similar puzzles arise, of course, if one looks for the episodes named by sentences containing the words 'if', 'not', 'probable', and 'possible'.

Our next task is to consider what are the fundamental 'categories' (in a sense similar to Kant's) that are necessarily presupposed in the 'language without extra-episodic words' whose properties we are studying. There seem to us to be four such categories, viz. space, time, number, and intensity. One records the position in space of the stimuli (normally, though not necessarily, using three-dimensional notions of space); one records their position in time; one records how many discrete objects there are, and one gives them values using the terms of physics—watts, lamberts, etc. (For convenience one may in fact speak, for example, of a 'green light', but in principle the word 'green' could be replaced by a physicist's description.) Similarly one records the place of the lever, the time at which the response occurs, the number of responses (lever pressings), and, if one wishes, the intensity with which the lever was pressed. The experimental situation can thus be fully described by the assigning of values, in the case of both stimulus and response, on the four scales in terms of which those four categories are quantified.

Organisms respond, of course, not to absolute stimulus values as such but to *differences* in stimulus value: an organism which had never been exposed to more than one value on a particular scale would not as a matter of logic have anything to discriminate. It would not be possible, for example, for a musician to display 'absolute pitch' unless he had at some stage been exposed to notes of *different* pitches. Similarly no verbalizing organism would be in a position to use the expressions 'to the left of' and 'before' unless more than one object was involved, nor would the concepts of *number* or *intensity* be applicable if there were only one number-word and only one word for describing the degree of intensity on a particular scale.

As things are, however, it is possible to vary the spatial layout of the stimulus mate ial and the temporal sequences of the events presented, while one can inclu le any number of objects and any degree of intensity within the limits of phys al practicability; and it is then an empirical matter whether the organism can respond to the differences. Space, time, number, and intensity are not, of course, *themselves* stimuli, at any rate not in any straightforward sense. (This again is one of Wittgenstein's 'say-what-you-like' situations.) One cannot ask a subject to make spatial or temporal discriminations without presenting him with *objects* in space and time, nor can one study his concepts of number or intensity unless one presents him with a number of *objects* or with stimulus material which can be quantified with regard to intensity.

It is worth noting that there are some very puzzling questions in this area connected with the concept of *time*. Stimuli in the ordinary sense act causally on the subject's receptors and hence on his nervous system, whereas space and time are not causal agents in this sense. Koffka (1935, p.440) considers the possibility that temporally successive events may stimulate *spatially* adjoining parts of the retina, but there seems no particular reason why such a pattern of stimulation should generate even awareness of space, let alone awareness of time, and Koffka's discussion seems to us to constitute an interesting statement of a problem rather than its solution. There are, it is true, idioms which imply that time has stimulus-like properties: it is 'like an ever-rolling stream' (cf. Smart, 1949, for an interesting discussion of this idiom); we consider what we would do 'if we had our time over again', a puzzling idea which seems to suggest that past time is like an object which one might lose and later (presumably at a different time) have restored, and we say that time is 'the great healer'; this not only suggests that healing will occur after lapse of time however much other things do or do not change, but even implies—erroneously, one must suppose—that it makes sense to speak of lapse of time independently of any events occurring in time such as the movement of a clock's hands or the beating of a heart. These idioms, however, like Koffka's speculation, seem to us to pose problems rather than to solve them. Part of the difficulty is certainly the lure of what may be called the 'cine-film analogy'. There are things which we can make a cine film do which are impossible in real life not because we lack the technical skill but because the concepts of success and failure are not applicable. Thus we could speed up the rate of presentation or slow it down; we could present parts of the film over again, and we could even run it backwards. It is misleading, however, to suppose that *time* could be speeded up or slowed down by some analogous process or, despite the familiar idiom, that it could be made to 'stand still'. Indeed, if such things were possible, a further time would be needed for measuring time's original speed and for 'timing' the standing-still period (cf. Dunne, 1939). Finally, a stimulus in the standard sense is something which can be varied in intensity or even switched off altogether, but a piece of apparatus which would switch *time* off is neither possible nor impossible.

It has commonly been supposed that operant psychology is committed to a programme which is 'behaviourist' at least in the sense of avoiding the use of mentalistic words. According to our view, however, what is required is rather the elimination of words which are extra-episodic. As it happens, many extra-episodic words, such as 'know' and 'recognize', are also mentalistic, but it is because they are extra-episodic and not because they are mentalistic that they are unserviceable in research. Indeed the verbs 'revoke' and 'garden', which are not 'mentalistic', would be unserviceable for similar reasons, while 'pressed the lever' is a serviceable expression because it has the positive virtue of being episodic, not because it avoids the alleged vice of being 'mentalistic'.

It is also supposed that if one requires human subjects to respond by pressing a lever one is somehow treating them as if they were rats! There is nothing in the least inhumane, however, about the ideal of a language without extra-episodic words, and indeed pressing the right lever at the right time could in some contexts be an extremely high-powered intellectual feat. It is of course true, as a matter of logic, that if frequency of responding over a period of time is set out on a cumulative record there are no concepts in such a situation which refer distinctively to humans as opposed to rats; but from this conceptual point nothing empirical follows as to the extent to which humans and rats are or are not alike. It is, of course, interesting that some mentalistic words, e.g. 'intend', though readily applicable to humans, are not easily used of rats (unless the rat is given human qualities, as in fiction); and it is not surprising, if a psychologist comes along and appears to say that mentalistic words should never be used of anybody (whether human or animal), that this proposal should be regarded as a threat. In fact what the operant psychologist is suggesting is not an insult to our humanity but a routine precaution which is necessary for effective research. This is a point to which we shall return in Chapter 8.

The important claim is that for certain purposes extra-episodic words are an encumbrance. This is because in research one wishes to hold the method of responding constant and simple. If the subject is given a complex reasoning task—for example, one of the puzzles about cans of water in the Terman intelligence test—and he fails, one does not know from his verbal response which component of the problem defeated him. If, however, he is required to press a lever, one can reasonably assume, unless he is paralysed, that the lever pressing as such was not too difficult for him; the whole burden of explanation can then be thrown on the stimulus conditions. This in fact is what is wanted, since in principle the experimenter may include in the stimulus conditions any combinations of stimuli that he pleases. If any more complicated response is required, e.g. one involving the use of language, all sorts of problems arise over questions of experimental design: perhaps the subject knew the answer but could not find the right word; perhaps his standards of what is 'green' or what is 'heavy' are different from the experimenter's, and so on. For this reason Harré (1971, p.116) seems to us to be mistaken in tilting at those psychologists who invent 'all sorts of ingenious ways of trying to find out about people by *not* asking them about their experiences', since if a subject responds verbally one cannot always be sure exactly what he is responding to. Moreover, if one wished to discover what are the changes which occur in response patterns when variables such as the intensity of a discriminative stimulus or the magnitude of a reinforcer are manipulated, it is hard to see how verbal responses could be as informative as lever presses. We are not, of course, saying that the former are never of use in psychological research, but only that those who choose the latter are not necessarily doing so out of doctrinaire allegiance to some questionable version of behaviouristic theory.

There may also be situations where it is convenient to ask a human subject to respond with the words 'yes' or 'no' or with the words 'same' or 'different'. Such procedure involves no departure from the ideal of a language without extra-episodic words, since a record of the subject's responses would in that case be a 'pure' account of what happened on a particular occasion, without any theorizing as to what might happen on other occasions. 'X emitted the response, "Different"'is just as much an account of a single episode as is 'X pressed the lever' and the variables controlling such a response could be equally open to experimental investigation.

It is worth emphasizing that an interesting feature of human lever pressing (and indeed of some animal lever pressing) is that its significance can sometimes by symbolic. It could quite well be true—to use ordinary idiom—that the human subject pressed the lever in order to signal or show something; and similarly it could be true that he knew the meaning of, say, the green light which the experimenter introduced at that point. As was pointed out in Chapter 5, it is no part of the operant programme to deny that the concept of *meaning* is important, though for research purposes it is insisted that sentences containing the expression 'knew the meaning of . . .' should be replaced with an account of what exactly the person said or did. Such an account is necessary in much the same way as it is necessary in a court of law to establish what the defendant *did* before one pronounces him 'guilty'.

It needs to be made clear, however, that the programme of eliminating extra-episodic words is a research device. It is useful, in other words, for those particular situations when we are doing research and where we require a method of responding which is constant and simple. In most other contexts extra-episodic words continue to be useful. It is perhaps helpful here to bring in a reference to evolutionary theory. Those linguistic expressions have survived, one may suggest, which make for ease of communication. Thus an extra-episodic word such as 'recognize' is useful because it enables us to say what a person has achieved and is likely to achieve without having to specify full details. For example, if it is in fact correct to say that X recognized Y, it is possible that X said 'Hello, Y!', that he made appropriate conversation to Y about his affairs, that he wrote 'There is Y' on a piece of paper, and so on; and for many purposes which of them he did is unimportant. In the case of human activity it is in fact often the significance of what was done which matters, not the precise bodily movements (including vocal and writing movements) by which the person did it. The movement in question may therefore have a significance far beyond the immediate situation; and, as we have seen already, it is an important charac-teristic of most mentalistic words that they are correctly used only if some or other of a whole complex of external (or extra-episodic) conditions are satisfied.

Finally, it is worth considering what could and could not be said in a language in which no extra-episodic words were allowed. Such a language would refer to events which could be tape-recorded or photographed, but any reference to the context in which such events occurred would be excluded: one could say *that* something happened but not *why* it happened. For example, one could record that X said 'Hello, Y!' on the stairs, but, unless there were subtle nuances in his tone of voice, there would be no means of telling whether or not he was saying it 'parrot-fashion'. Again, there are a variety of ways, as things are, by which X can demonstrate that he knows his six times table, but there would be no way of indicating that correct recitation, putting right another person's mistake, and saying 'Forty-eight' when asked 'What is eight time six?' were near-equivalent responses from which the same inference could be drawn about what X might do on other occasions. All these considerations exhibit the richness and complexity of ordinary language. Such complexity is all to the good in many contexts; but if one is doing certain kinds of psychological research it may be undesirable to commit oneself beyond the here-and-now, and therefore records of lever presses are in these circumstances of more help than sentences containing the words 'know', 'recognize', 'learn', and 'forget'. In this sense, therefore, it is necessary for any psychologist to be an analytical behaviourist, since in suitable contexts it is essential that these words are translated out. The reason why they need to be translated out, however, is not because they are mentalistic but because they are extra-episodic.

Chapter 7

Can a Strong Version of Operant Psychology be Defended?

There is a story told of an aspiring writer who submitted some of his work to an expert for criticism. He was told that what he had written was 'both good and original'. The sequel, however, was less flattering. 'Unfortunately', said the expert, 'the parts which are good are not original and the parts which are original are not good.'

We suspect that there are critics who feel similarly about operant psychology. Scriven (1956, p. 88), for instance, asserts that 'Skinner's position on almost every issue admits of two interpretations—one of them exciting, controversial and practically indefensible; the other moderately interesting, widely accepted and very plausible'. On this showing the exciting claims made on behalf of operant psychology are incorrect and the correct things (for instance, that psychologists need to be rigorous in their search for controlling variables) not particularly exciting.

There are, on the other hand, those who would insist that operant techniques have provided psychology with a radically new approach and placed it, once and for all, on a firm scientific basis. Platt (1973) even goes so far as to use the word 'revolution'.

'There is no doubt', he writes,

> that Skinner's approach is leading to a radical reprogramming of psychology. Until recently, psychology has seemed to be standing still for lack of a general organizing principle. Freud's formulations have been greatly discredited by recent experiments; Pearsonian measurements and correlations usually do not show us how to do anything; personality 'traits' and even intelligence tests are under fire; the theories of 'drives' could not even explain such compulsive behaviour as gambling; the great learning theorists did not show us how to teach faster; the 'classical conditioning' methods of the early behaviourists have been of little use in schools or child training, or even animal training; and the schools of loving responsiveness, group therapy, and 'peak experiences' have been warm and inspiring but not very scientific.
>
> Into this sea of ineffectiveness, Skinner has brought, over the last thirty-

five years, a technique and theory of 'operant conditioning' and behavior modification that has transformed every behavioral problem and approach. His method can speed up animal learning by 10 to 100 times (Skinner, 1959; Pryor, 1969), can be used to improve behavior in psychiatric wards (Ayllon and Azrin, 1968), cure problems such as bed-wetting and stuttering that have resisted psychiatric treatment (Ulrich *et al.*, 1966; Krasner and Ullman, 1965), cure disruptive or delinquent behavior (Tharp and Wetzel, 1970), and can double the learning rate in schools from kindergarten through college (Skinner, 1968; Whaley and Malott, 1971). It can be used for self-control of unwanted habits (Ulrich *et al.*, 1966; Stuart and Davis, 1970; Whaley and Malott, 1971), and even for yoga-like voluntary control of heartbeat, blood pressure, and other autonomic functions that had been supposed to be beyond conscious control (DiCara and Miller, 1968; Miller, 1969).

It is evidently important for us—and for everyone—to understand just how such a powerful method works and what it implies about biology and human nature. (Platt, 1973, pp. 23–24)

How much, then, can and should be claimed on behalf of operant psychology? Few would dispute that it has produced some elegant experiments and that in certain applied fields it has had some measure of success. The present chapter, however, is concerned to ask whether there is any justification for claims which are considerably stronger than this. Is it correct, for instance, to speak, like Platt (1973), of a 'revolution'? And, if so, does this mean that other approaches to psychology are somehow discredited?

What we ourselves would like to see is the progressive disappearance of any kind of boundary between operant psychology and other kinds of psychology. This is not to suggest that the operant approach should remain unchanged and that those lost sheep who do their psychology in other ways should be invited into the operant fold. On the contrary, operant psychology may itself need to undergo all kinds of adjustments and modifications, while those who at present would disclaim any pretension to be doing operant work may, we hope, in the future be willing to modify their procedures as a result of the insights which the operant approach can offer.

Meanwhile it seems to us important not to underestimate the claims which are logically required. Platt's use of the word 'revolution' is in our view no mere rhetorical exaggeration; and in this chapter we shall try to show both that certain lines of investigation could be followed more effectively if operant concepts were taken more seriously and that other kinds of research are too ineffective in their present form to be worth pursuing.

To establish our case we shall consider in turn four specific areas of research. These are: (1) research involving model building in the study of memory, (2) research in physiological psychology, (3) research involving correlational techniques and their derivatives, and (4) research in educational psychology. We shall argue—more, perhaps, in sorrow than in anger—that research under

(1) and (2) could be considerably strengthened by a shift towards operant ways of thinking, whereas in the case of (3) we shall attempt, somewhat more polemically, to expose what we regard as serious methodological weaknesses, while in the case of (4) we shall suggest that claims to scientific expertise on the part of some of those who practise research in the educational field must of necessity be thoroughly suspect.

To argue in defence of this 'strong' version of operant psychology may at first glance seem arrogant and sectarian. The alternative, however, may turn out to be no more than a kind of amiable open-mindedness resulting from failure to think things through to their logical limits. If, none the less, we give the impression in this chapter of being unjustifiably polemical, we should like to make clear that our attack is not directed against those psychologists who on an informed basis decide that for their particular purpose operant concepts are inappropriate. In so far as we are adversely critical, it is of those psychologists who do not know what methods are available, who ask a particular kind of question because they are unaware of the alternative questions which could be asked, and who claim expertise even though they do not and cannot know what are the controlling variables.

It is no part of our thesis to suggest that operant psychology is in some way a substitute for other branches of psychology or that, for instance, a developmental psychologist should abandon developmental psychology *in favour of* operant psychology. Such a claim rests on the incorrect assumption that operant psychology and developmental psychology are sub-divisions within the total area of psychology. It is perhaps less misleading to think in terms of operant *techniques*, and our thesis is that such techniques can help psychologists, whatever their interests, to do their job better.

By the same argument, it is not our purpose in defending a 'strong' version of operant psychology to disparage psychotherapy or claim that it should on all occasions be superseded by behaviour therapy. It may well be that in the psychotherapy situation knowledge of the controlling variables is hard to come by; it may even be true that some practising psychotherapists are not as stringent as they should be in checking the correctness of what they believe about controlling variables, and it is certainly important, as Skinner (1956) has shown, that sentences about superegos, etc., should in principle be capable of being translated into sentences about behaviour. Those who say such things, however, cannot with any justification be accused of 'disparaging psychotherapy'. Our suggestion is rather that operant techniques can contribute positively. The psychotherapy situation is in fact one which the 'behaviour-being-reinforced' formula fits extremely well; and the decision for the psychotherapist is, on this view, that of determining what behaviour to reinforce. Reinforcers might be, for example, such remarks as 'Can you say some more?' or 'This seems important to you'. The operant approach forces psychotherapists to clarify their objectives, since it confronts them with the question, 'What behaviour must the organism display if the treatment is to be regarded as successful?'; and it also serves as an antidote against unwitting reinforcement of those responses which fit a particular scheme, e.g. the Freudian. This is a far cry from claiming that psychotherapy is a waste of time. Whether in fact it must be adjudged a waste of time depends largely on what it achieves; and, as we shall see more fully in Chapter 9, this is an empirical matter.

In short, then, our defence of a 'strong' version of operant psychology is in effect an appeal to psychologists, whatever their special interests, to take the concepts of operant psychology seriously, on the grounds that they will be missing something important if they fail to do so.

1. Most of those psychologists who study memory at the present time assume that the right question to ask is, 'What model of memory is the most correct or appropriate?' The following passage from D. A. Norman aptly illustrates this view:

> Naming something 'attention', something else 'perception' and yet something else 'learning' adds to our vocabulary but not to our knowledge. The psychologist will not be satisfied until he can point to a specific process—that sequence of operations which performs transformations and makes decisions on sensory information—and identify this as a mechanism of attention . . . The ultimate in specification is a model which describes in detail the operations which underlie attention, perception, learning, and memory . . . The systematic investigation of psychological processes has only just begun. (Norman, 1969, p. 2)

Such talk, we suggest, can helpfully be regarded as a statement of programme. Norman is implicitly commending the use of a particular set of concepts: research is to be described in terms, for example, of 'sequence of operations', 'transformations', and 'decision making' (in a technical sense). The implied analogy is with the processing of information by computers; and experiments on memory are to be regarded as ways of testing different theories as to how information is 'stored' and 'retrieved'.

This conceptual scheme is in many ways unlike the operant one and, in our opinion, far less satisfactory. We are not, of course, saying that the experiments performed by Norman and others under its influence are of no value. The actual formulation which we have quoted, however, is conceptually confused: what Norman says is at best unnecessary and at worst seriously misleading.

When people claim to be studying the operations which 'underlie' attention, perception, learning, and memory, it is doubtful whether any clear meaning can be attached to the word 'underlie'. Even if it could, however, no reason is given for preferring the study of 'underlying' processes to that of overt ones. If X sees Y, whom he knows, and says 'Hello, Y!', there are many psychologists who would wish to say that 'information' about Y had earlier been 'stored' in X's brain and had now been 'retrieved'. It is possible, however, with greater economy of terms and less theoretical commitment, to say that, presented with this particular stimulus, X emitted the verbal response 'Hello, Y!', and to go on to investigate the conditions under this that response reliably occurs in the presence of those stimuli.

Norman also appears to have overlooked the point that the verbs 'attend', 'perceive', 'learn', and 'remember' do not all have the same logic. It makes as little sense to say 'I have been doing some remembering' as to say 'I have been doing some knowing', and although a person may attend or fail to attend to what he is doing it does not follow that two processes were involved, the first that of doing the activity in question, the second that of attending. To suggest that one should study the processes *underlying* this act of attention is thus doubly misleading: in the first place, to believe in the existence of such an act is to misconstrue the logic of the word 'attend'; and, second, if *per impossibile* there were such acts it would surely be more sensible to study them in their own right rather than try to study something else of which they are allegedly manifestations. Instead, one needs, after the manner of Wittgenstein, Austin, and Ryle, to study how the words 'attend', 'perceive', 'learn', and 'remember' function in the hands of those ordinary unsophisticated speakers of the English language who know nothing about 'underlying processes'. The result of such a study inevitably leads one to question the assumption that all these four words alike stand for 'processes' and hence to question the further assumption that some kind of 'mechanism' is necessarily involved when these alleged processes occur. With the operant conceptual scheme all this Cloud-cuckoo-land disappears, and one starts instead with a simple statement of what was the stimulus and what the subject said or did.

It may be objected that to talk in this way is to underestimate the importance of theory. 'We still need to know', it might be said, 'not just *that* particular responses occur but *why* they occur. We need to see how these responses fit into a total system and how this system works.' It is not clear, however, from such an objection what kind of explanation is being sought. There is an important sense of 'explain' in which one can be said to have explained an action if one has specified the necessary and sufficient conditions for its occurrence; and if this is the sense intended then clearly no reference to underlying 'mechanisms' is necessary. For example, it is a fully sufficient answer to the question 'Why did he write "fifty-six"?' to say 'He was asked, "What is eight times seven?"' In so far as this answer is incomplete, what is needed is some further indication of the circumstances, for example that nothing had happened in the time immediately preceding the stimulus to cause him to behave differently. In such a context questions, for instance, as to whether the response 'fifty-six' occurred as a result of processes in 'long-term memory' or processes in 'short-term memory' do not arise.

It may still be objected, however, that other kinds of explanation are possible. So indeed they are. Those who look for explanations in terms of storage and retrieval mechanisms, however, seem to us to have two choices open to them. Either they wish to make claims about how the nervous system works or they do not. If the former, then they are advocating the procedures of physiological psychology, in which case the considerations adduced in the next section become relevant. If the latter, they would presumably wish to claim that their investigations are designed to discover what kind of principles are presupposed by the behavioural data. Now it is arguable that our existing knowledge is in fact scanty and that model building is therefore premature; but even if this point is not pressed, there is still a difficulty. Since on this showing no claims are being made of a physiological kind, the only way of checking the validity of a particular model would need to be in terms of more comprehensive and detailed studies of behaviour. In that case, however, it is the behaviour itself which is the basic datum, and the function of any postulated 'model' is simply to suggest further ways by which such behaviour could be studied. We have in fact come across many experiments where the investigator has claimed to be studying storage and retrieval of information but which in our view have been admirable experiments of an operant kind!

2. We have noticed a certain ambivalence on the part of operant psychologists towards physiological psychology. Perhaps this is because of the relatively close relationship between the two. There is no corresponding love–hate relationship between, say, an operant psychologist and one who practises psychometrics, since they are too far apart to have any relationship at all. In the last resort, however, no very firm distinction seems possible between observation of behaviour and so-called 'physiological measurement': to study activity in the heart, the nerves, or the kidneys is not different in any radical way from studying the results of activity by the hands (lever pressing or writing), by the vocal chords (speaking), by the eyes (staring), by the legs (walking), and so on. Those more gross movements which are immediately detectable by an observer are called 'behaviour', whereas those movements which either take place inside the body or are too slight to be detectable without special instrumentation are thought to be the concern not of the behavioural psychologist but of the physiologist. This, however, is plainly no more than a rough-and-ready distinction of limited significance.

From the arguments put forward by Skinner (1950) one might conclude that in a science of behaviour physiological investigations are seldom necessary. They would in fact be required only in those rare situations where an organism's behaviour was under the control solely of events within its own body. In most cases, therefore, it is possible to correlate input and output without considering what happens to the stimulus material when it has passed inside the organism's skin. It is interesting, however, that Skinner does not in fact lay much stress on this argument, his main comment on physiological psychology being simply that it is not very far advanced; and he therefore concludes that its findings are of 'limited usefulness' (1953, p. 29) in the prediction and control of behaviour. Much depends here, of course, on what one judges to be the likelihood of any major breakthrough with regard to the neurological basis of learning; but it is arguable that suitably designed operant experiments at least for the present have better prospects. It is worth adding, as an *argumentum ad hominem*, that in our judgement some would-be physiological psychologists have received very inadequate training in physiology and that if one wishes to draw conclusions of a physiological kind adequate background knowledge is essential.

It may still be suggested, however, that the teaching of many different kinds of skill can be improved when physiological findings are taken into account. Whether this is in fact so is of course an empirical matter, and we have no wish to prejudge future findings. We do wonder, however, if the likelihood of success is as great as some people have supposed; and in this connection we should like to comment on an important point of method. It is sometimes possible that people who claim to be applying physiological knowledge in the teaching of skills are misleading themselves. If a pupil is receiving tuition in lawn tennis, for instance, or music, it is quite common to hear the teacher come up with some (decidedly speculative) physiology on the basis of which he tells him to hit the ball in some particular way or do a certain kind of finger exercise. Since an experienced teacher knows that doing things in this way will in fact lead to success, it is tempting to suppose that his physiological claims are thereby supported. In fact, however, the 'experiment' is purely behavioural: the pupil is responding to verbal instructions which the teacher has found to be effective in the past.

To sum up this section, our thesis is not that the achievements to date of physiological psychologists should be belittled. We do wonder, however, if in the next few decades more progress may be made through behavioural studies than through physiological ones.

3. It seems to us that in practice many correlational studies in psychology are of limited power and utility. In studies of delinquent behaviour, for instance, one is continually told that there is a correlation between crime and certain disadvantages in home background. As Sprott (1952, p. 256) has aptly pointed out, however, we are not always in a position to know how 'the factors which are brought out by large-scale study affect the individual victim'. The mistake here, as any operant psychologist would immediately point out, is to suppose that someone can come up with *the* way to change a delinquent personality. To quote Sidman (1960, p. 49), 'A sufficient number of experiments have demonstrated that the behaviour of an individual subject is an orderly function of a large number of so-called independent variables.' Instead, therefore, of looking for correlations between, for instance, delinquency and home background and then attempting to make statements about 'the' delinquent in general, one would look at *particular* delinquents and try to discover in a particular case what stimuli had made—or would make in the future—particular behaviour more probable. One would ask whether society was not unwittingly reinforcing the wrong type of behaviour and consider what was happening not just in some kind of once- or twice-weekly training session but in the environment as a whole. With such enquiries the need for correlation coefficients may well not arise.

There is the same kind of limitation in the case of factor analytic studies of intelligence and personality. From the nature of the case such studies can tell us only what kinds of characteristic do or do not 'go together'. Without supplementation from other kinds of enquiry it is impossible as a matter of logic that one could acquire knowledge of the relevant controlling variables. Thus one might account for patterns or regularities in a matrix of correlation coefficients by postulating, for example, a 'k-factor' of which particular tests were to some extent a measure, and one might thereby be in a position to predict, at least above the chance level, how particular subjects would behave in response to other tests with a high 'k' loading. If, however, one is concerned to influence the subject's performance or train him to respond correctly to these and similar tests, something very much more is needed than a collection of unsystematized associations at the better-than-chance level. One needs to know what stimuli will make particular changes in responding more probable.

There is a danger, too, that if one uses factor analysis too readily—and this is true also of other statistical techniques such as analysis of variance—one may become uncritically naïve about the value of the original scores on which the calculations are based. A score, after all, is no more than a notation which relates to some of the things, not necessarily the most important ones, which the subject did. In these circumstances statistical techniques lead one further and further from asking the important operant-type questions, 'What did the subject do?' and 'What are the variables which control such behaviour?'

Finally, factor analytic studies are usually based on test scores which indicate how a person scored *on a particular occasion*, whereas operant techniques make possible a study of the subject's behaviour over time. This does not of itself prove the superiority of operant techniques for all occasions, since this would be like arguing that cine photographs were always 'better' than static ones. But it is hard to believe that 'test scores' and the resultant statistical manipulations have much of a future as a contribution to pure science now that techniques for studying behaviour over time are being widely developed. Careful research workers in the psychometric field have of course always emphasized the need for checking test–retest reliability, but there has been a tendency to regard variability as a tiresome complication rather than as an object of study in its own right. Here, too, a change of orientation seems called for.

To sum up this section (in an admittedly provocative way), we should like to suggest that psychology would be better off if there were a truce on the use of the correlation coefficient for the next 10 years!

4. From the research point of view educational psychology seems to us to be in a very sorry state. We are not, of course, in any way disputing the practical and administrative skills of many educational psychologists; but these, in our judgement, are the result largely of good sense and experience rather than of any distinctive specialist expertise. Indeed, ironically enough, it is in the area where there is commonly supposed to be some distinctive expertise, viz. that of educational measurement, that the weakness of present-day educational psychology stands most exposed. If the central thesis of this chapter is right, advances can be made not by bigger and better surveys—in which, for example, IQs, reading ages, and spelling ages are investigated on an even larger scale—but by reflection on a few basic operant principles.

To suppose that educational surveys are the stuff out of which any serious scientific breakthrough could arise is undoubtedly mistaken. It is as though, after a storm, people set themselves to count the number of tiles which had fallen off the roofs of houses in a particular area—and then solemnly declared that they were doing physics! It is, of course, true that the behaviour of such slates can be accounted for in terms of the laws of physics, but a physicist who did this kind of counting would rightly be condemned by his colleagues as out of date. We are not saying that it is a waste of time to count such slates; indeed this might be a very necessary exercise for local government officials concerned with problems of housing, but it would still need to be distinguished from physics! Similarly if, say, the education authority in a country borough wants figures for illiteracy in its area, records of how many words from a standarized test each child of a given age in the area spelled correctly or otherwise may well be of help. If activities such as these are called 'psychology', however, it is important to be clear that they are different from those enquiries where a systematic attempt is made to analyse the relevant variables.

It is, of course, no objection to the concepts of *reading age* and *spelling age* that they involve an abstraction from behaviour. To require a subject to press a lever involves similar abstraction. It is quite reasonable for particular purposes to say that one will limit one's studies and record only the subject's lever-pressing responses and not, for instance, the number of times he draws in breath. In the case of traditional reading and spelling tests, however, most investigators seem to have accepted uncritically that a dichotomous classification of behaviour is the only thing needed. Either the behaviour satisfies certain pre-existing criteria (in other words the word is read or spelled correctly) or it does not. With this approach one may have thrown away large amounts of potential information before the research has even started.

If only such investigators could be persuaded, instead of preparing large tables of statistics, to look at a single child and look at him in more detail! No one, surely, who has seen a child struggling with a reading or spelling task can doubt that many extremely interesting responses are also very difficult to score.

If one tries to correlate reading and spelling ages with other factors, e.g. home background, one is still not isolating the variables which *control* reading and spelling behaviour. If there turns out to be a correlation between parental income and reading age it is not clear that the best way of improving the child's reading age is to pay his parents more money or even tell them to go and earn some more. Again, few in educational circles would dispute the wisdom of trying, where possible, to persuade parents to give encouragement to children over their reading; but this conclusion does not need to be bolstered by elaborate surveys using correlation coefficients (which in any case might not produce findings relevant to the needs of *individual* children), and a psychologist whose 'expertise' led him to come out in favour of parental encouragement could fairly be accused of telling people what they already know.

Moreover, without an operant analysis, it is difficult to recognize clearly the relationship between reading and spelling. As things are at present, some organizations put on courses for specifically the teaching of reading, without, apparently, any adequate appreciation of the need for considering spelling at the same time. In an operant approach one considers in detail possible ways of presenting the stimulus-material and possible 'operants' in the sense of ways in which the subject is invited to respond. Sometimes, for instance, the stimulus could be presented visually, sometimes auditorily; sometimes the subject could be required to respond orally, sometimes in writing, in the one case providing the experimenter with an auditory stimulus and in the other case providing him with a visual stimulus. Other senses could be brought in, for instance if braille were used or if someone were to trace the shape of letters in the air or shut his eyes while a word is 'written' on the back of his hand. Moreover, since both written and vocal responses are possible to both visual and auditory stimuli, a 2 × 2 table can be set up, with different verbal labels according to the four different combinations shown in Figure 2. It is interesting that no technical terms are needed in any of the four 'cells' since ordinary language has words which exactly distinguish the four types of situation.

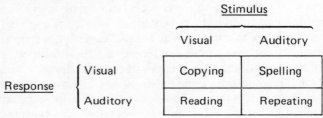

Figure 2

This figure, although from the nature of the case it cannot establish anything demonstratively, at least suggests the possibility that it may be mistaken to limit oneself to the study of reading on its own. It reminds one, for example, that it may be possible to improve a child's reading by teaching him to spell, and it suggests that one might helpfully investigate whether those who have difficulty in reading also have difficulty in copying and repeating (which in fact they sometimes do). Once again we are not attacking any informed decision, e.g. the deliberate choice to study reading on its own; but we are attacking those who claim to be authorities on reading without even knowing that this kind of operant approach is available.

The concept of *IQ* has of course been criticized on many counts. Here we shall limit ourselves to specifically 'operant' kinds of objection. On the traditional view, if a child of a certain age has a particular score, then certain more advanced items are 'too difficult' for him. To an operant psychologist, on the other hand, the appropriate questions are: 'What kinds of behaviour do you wish the subject to emit?' and 'What are the controlling variables which will lead to such behaviour?' To quote Skinner (1969, p. 80), 'The statement that a given type of organism or an organism of a given age "cannot solve a given kind of problem" is meaningless until the speaker has specified the programs which have been tried and considered the possibility that better ones may be designed,' In addition, from the way in which the stimuli are presented in an intelligence test any possibility of *controlling* the subject's responses must be absent. This is because all the stimuli are complex ones and there is no means of ensuring what the components are. In the Terman 'cans of water' tests, for instance, one component is that the child should be able to say the number-series and operate in various ways with numerical relationships, e.g. by knowing that $9 + 4 = 13$; another component is that he should be able to select one particular relationship from all those which he knows; a further component is that he should be able to respond appropriately to the words 'not guessing the amount', and so on. With an operant approach one would try to isolate these components out and reinforce each individually: when appropriate responding is achieved on one component on its own, one would repeat the procedure for other components, repeat it again for two components in conjuction, and so on. Quite apart from any ethical or social objections to statements purporting to say what a child's 'ceiling' is, there is the fundamental objection that, unless suitable 'programs' (in Skinner's sense) are tried, the statement that a particular level represents the child's 'ceiling' may turn out to be false.

There is yet a further objection, from the operant point of view, to much current educational psychology. One of the experimental designs in common use is the 'two groups' design, in which the performance of an experimental group is compared with that of a control group. A more refined version involves the use of matched pairs, though the basic principle is the same. The logic here is impeccable. Given that an investigator wishes to investigate the influence of M and that M cannot be isolated on its own, he produces it along with A, B, and C; if he now compares the differences between the combination ABCM and the combination ABC on its own, he can of course be sure that any differences between the two groups are associated with the presence of M. In practice, however, the A of the one group may not be exactly the same as the A of the other; matching is seldom adequate and many differences both between and within subjects may be unaccounted for. In contrast, the kind of design which is often used in operant work is free from this kind of objection. Here the subject is used as his own control; there is a baseline phase, an experimental phase (in which a new variable is introduced) and a reversal phase (where the new variable is withdrawn), and one can say with a high degree of confidence that any changes in the experimental phase are the result of the variable whose influence one has chosen to study.

Once again we do not wish to advocate the doctrinaire view that the experimental-versus-control-group design should never be used. Much may depend on what is practicable, and much will certainly depend on the kinds of statement which one wishes to make at the end. What is disturbing is the apparent failure on the part of some educational research workers to realize that alternative techniques are available. If the objectives are prediction and control the three-phase design is likely in many contexts to be more effective; and if at any time another design is chosen this should be the result of careful consideration of available alternatives.

An experienced parent or teacher may well know a large amount about the variables which influence children's behaviour; so, indeed, may an experienced educational psychologist. The great weakness of present-day educational psychology, however, is that additional knowledge, based on systematic research, is extremely scanty; and educational surveys in their present form are at best a kind of operant psychology *manqué* since they do not attempt to study the relevant variables in isolation. We are not, of course, accusing any educational research workers of being intentionally dishonest, but we suspect that some of them may have overestimated the scientific value of what the educational survey in its present form can achieve.

It has not been our purpose in this chapter to foreclose any area from psychological research. Our thesis is rather that the operant conceptual scheme can help psychologists to ask appropriate questions and discover the right methods of answering them. Those who fail to take operant concepts seriously are thus depriving themselves of insights which could make their research more effective. If this thesis counts as a 'strong' one, then a 'strong' version of operant psychology is in our view fully defensible.

Chapter 8

On the Charge of Being 'Soulless'

'Modern psychology', writes Koch (1964, pp. 37–38), 'has projected an image of man which is as demeaning as it is simplistic.' Similar criticisms have been voiced both within and without the mainstream of present-day psychology (cf. Koestler, 1967; Guntrip, 1972; Joynson, 1973). To some people, it seems, there is an 'establishment' in psychology which, in its desire to insist on full scientific rigour, robs the subject of its interest and humanity.

On this showing, operant psychology is commonly thought to be on the side of the 'establishment'. Indeed, to its more severe critics it represents the epitome of an uncompromising materialism, its insensitivity matched only by the arrogance with which its exponents proclaim their rectitude. It is charged with being a tough-minded creed which assumes that humans are basically no different from rats and are influenced solely by the desire for food, water, and sexual satisfaction; some of its practices are suspect on ethical grounds, as when its adherents administer severe electric shocks or fail to comfort a child who is crying for fear of reinforcing the 'wrong' kind of behaviour; it denies that there is freedom of choice; its research fails to attach importance to the factor of human relationships; it does not allow for the appreciation of art, music, and literature, and it has no sympathetic understanding of those 'friends' to man, as Wordsworth calls them,

> . . . exultations, agonies,
> And love, and man's unconquerable mind.

In short, operant psychology is accused of being a 'soulless' enterprise.

In rejecting this charge we shall not, of course, be committing a *volte face* and proposing a return to Cartesian dualism. A pianist, well known to one of the authors, was once told, 'You play with soul!' What makes such a statement true, however, is not the presence of some non-physical forces additional to those physically measurable forces which are transferred from the fingers to the keyboard. When people play with soul they display extra sensitivity or powers of discrimination, e.g. by placing subtle emphasis on a particular note in relation to the preceding one. The difference between 'soulful' and mechanical playing does not consist in the fact that only physical forces are present in the latter whereas forces undetectable by physics are present in the former; it is rather that in 'soulful' playing the forces transferred from fingers to keyboard are of a special complex kind. There is much about human nature which is unknown, and this of course gives legitimate cause for humility and wonder; but it is hard to see what sense can be attached to asserting that there are forces at work which are unknowable in principle, and even if there were such forces we do not see why human personality should be additionally deserving of respect as a result. To have reservations about the merits of Cartesian dualism is not to be 'soulless' in any sense which implies lack of sensitivity.

The objections which have led to the charge of 'soullessness' can conveniently be classified under three heads, viz. (1) objections on empirical grounds, (2) objections on ethical grounds, (3) objections on conceptual grounds. We shall consider each of these in turn. It will not be our purpose to defend all that has been done in the name of 'operant psychology' in the past: if there have been ethical malpractices, then clearly this is to be regretted, and if some psychologists either by their actions or their writings have shown themselves to be insensitive, this is to be regretted also. As a point of logic, however, there seems to us nothing in the operant approach to necessitate 'soullessness' in any objectionable sense; and indeed many such alleged criticisms of operant psychology appear to be the result of misunderstanding rather than to be expressions of genuine disagreement. If X says to Y, 'I disagree with you because you do A and believe B', and Y replies, 'I neither do A nor believe B', the word 'disagreement' is scarcely in place! Much of the argument in this chapter will in effect be devoted to the removal of misunderstandings.

1. It is sometimes suggested that the claims made by those using operant techniques have been exaggerated and that the alleged regularities in human and animal behaviour occur at most only in the special restricted conditions of the laboratory. For example, it has been argued that failure by operant psychologists to take ethological work seriously has led to faulty generalizations on questions of fact. Here, by way of illustration, is an extract from a recent review of a book about Konrad Lorenz:

> The notion of 'innate' behavioural tendencies runs counter to certain prejudices of the empirical tradition on which scientific method is supposedly based and, though apparently irrefutably established by Lorenz's wonderfully patient observations, continues to be disparaged by, notably, the Skinnerian school of behaviourists.
> Skinner believes that living creatures are entirely conditioned by the world into which they are born and carry no genomic protocols by way of prior instruction. (*Sunday Times*, 18 January 1976)

These polemical remarks, however, are simply misinformed. Not only do they misrepresent Skinner, who has in fact made clear (personal communication) that he is by no means opposed to ethological studies; they show in addition that the writer is under a misapprehension: he has failed to appreciate that it is possible to study the ways in which stimuli from the environment reinforce certain kinds of behaviour without disputing the existence or importance of genetic make-up.

In any case, as has already been pointed out, the validity of the operant approach does not stand or fall with the results of *particular* experiments. If it turned out, for instance, that one could not legitimately make general statements about what is likely to reinforce children with severe mental handicap it still would not follow that the concept of a *reinforcer* is no use; and even if in a particular area the facts turned out to be very complex it would still be very strange policy to *discourage* people from looking for reinforcers.

One can admittedly conceive of a world where there were fewer regularities. For instance, it would be harder to make accurate predictions if, like Alice, one played croquet with flamingos instead of mallets, or if, like the Mikado's victims, one had to play billiards

On a cloth untrue
With a twisted cue
And elliptical billiard balls;

and, extrapolating from this, one can imagine a situation where even those croquet or billiard balls which were correctly struck nevertheless strayed from their course in accordance with no known law. Even in such outlandish circumstances, however, it would be difficult to dispense with the physical notion of 'force'. Similarly, even if organisms behaved more unpredictably than in fact they do, the concept of a *reinforcer* would not, for that reason, turn out to be useless. Indeed, even if a sophisticated human subject set out in his responding to 'refute operant psychology' it is impossible as a matter of logic that he could ever do so. However he responded—for instance, if he pressed the lever at completely random time intervals without regard to the stimuli presented—it would still be possible to ask what were the conditions controlling such behaviour; and in this particular case one might expect to find that he had had some previous hostile encounter with the experimenter and had made the explicit verbalization, 'I am determined to prove him wrong.' The issue here is not *whether* his behaviour shows orderly relations but what orderly relations can be found.

Some introductory textbooks may perhaps give a misleading impression with regard to reinforcement. Thus one commonly reads that reinforcers are 'such things as food, drink, sex, etc.'; and it is difficult to avoid the suspicion that the use of the word 'etc.' indicates that the writer is unsure how to continue the list. In point of fact it is possible in logic that any energy change in the environment could function as a reinforcer if the conditions were right. Moreover it is quite unnecessary to assume that all reinforcers must have some one property in common, or even several properties in common, and it seems likely on empirical grounds that they do not. A particular stimulus may reinforce on one occasion and not on another, and on yet another occasion a quite different stimulus may be reinforcing. To search for a common property possessed by all reinforcers is like looking for a common property shared by everything that is said to be 'good'. To quote Hare (1952), 'Good cacti seem to have little in common with good chronometers, and good chronometers with good cricket bats (p. 97) . . . 'The primary function of the word "good" is to commend' (p. 127).

Particularly troublesome is the alleged complementary class of stimuli which are non-reinforcers. The phenomenon of conditioned reinforcement is well known: these 'neutral' stimuli, when paired with food, are found to affect behaviour much as food affects it. Consequently, when a supposed neutral stimulus appears to have a reinforcing effect upon behaviour it is assumed to have been related to food (or water or sex) at some time in the past. But what of music, art, and books? It is hard to suppose that they have acquired their effect through association with basic biological functions.

Such a view is, of course, a crude form of biological theory which can readily be shown to be false. It is not plausible that people should brave cold and wet London evenings to go to the opera if what was entailed was association of the music and the stage in the dim and distant past with food, water, or sex. Indeed, in the light of what we know about conditioned reinforcement and deprivation, we might expect, on this view, that the opera house would be filled with the hungry, the thirsty, and the sex-starved, and that the satiated would stay at home. A brief look at the Covent Garden audience on any night will give the lie to such a supposition!

Similar conclusions can be drawn from the behaviour of children. It is not an uncommon experience of mothers to find that they have to reward eating by, for example, being delighted when the child eats, whereas there seem to be very few occasions when some other behaviour of the child can be rewarded by giving food, or even, in many cases, so-called preferred foods such as sweets. There are many instances in the literature where sweets are found to be ineffective or weak reinforcers.

It follows from all this that the above 'stereotype' of the operant psychologist is unjustified. Anyone, of course, can be wrong on an empirical question; but it is unhelpful to attribute mistaken empirical views to 'operant psychologists' in general and then point out how wrong they are!

2. The objections mentioned at the start of this chapter, in so far as they relate to ethical issues, can conveniently be classified under six headings. Thus it might be argued: (a) that 'behaviour modifiers' treat people as though they were rats, (b) that they fail to respect the patient's right to freedom, (c) that sometimes the methods of training are painful, for instance when they involve the administration of electric shock, (d) that in their anxiety not to reinforce troublesome behaviour they may fail to respond helpfully to patients with genuine needs, (e) that they sometimes trick their patients into responding in particular ways, and (f) that they themselves decide what is good for the patient instead of letting him decide for himself.

In what follows we shall not discuss the empirical question of whether particular operant psychologists (or would-be operant psychologists) are to be found who are guilty of any of these malpractices. We shall be concerned rather with the conceptual question of whether there is anything in the operant approach which supports or encourages any ethically dubious activities, and we shall try to show that there is not.

Objection (a) is clearly the result of misunderstanding. As has been shown in Chapter 6, it is often convenient with human subjects no less than with animal subjects to use the lever press or some similar behaviour as the unit of study, and the same procedure (investigation of controlling variables) and the same concepts can be used whether human or animal subjects are involved. It does not follow, however, that an operant psychologist is committed to supposing that men are no different from rats; and the exact nature of the differences is, of course, an empirical matter.

(b) With regard to the patient's right to freedom one can again see how a wrong impression may have been created. It is widely supposed that operant psychology is 'determinist' in character (whatever this means); and since belief in freedom is held to be incompatible with belief in determinism, the impression is presumably created that an operant psychologist cannot from the nature of the case take the need for freedom seriously. The issue of determinism will be considered in Chapter 10. All that need be said here is that as a matter of logic there can be nothing in the operant approach that would establish that people never have free choices. It seems to us plain that sometimes they do and sometimes they do not; the issue is again an empirical one.

Even if this were not so, however, philosophical conclusions about determinism would still be logically independent of statements about how much freedom is desirable, whether in a country, a classroom, a hospital ward, or anywhere else. 'Freedom' in this sense means 'absence of coercive control', and those who use operant concepts are not logically committed to believing that either a large or a small amount of such control is desirable.

Moreover if it were shown empirically that in certain circumstances coercive control was an effective method of achieving particular results, one would have to weigh the loss of freedom against the resultant gains. There is nothing new, however, in such a dilemma, and it has very little to do with operant psychology as such. If, for example, one is sure on empirical grounds that the wearing of seat-belts decreases the probability of damage when a car is involved in an accident, one still has to weigh this gain against possible losses that would allegedly be involved if the wearing of seat-belts were made compulsory. In point of fact the evidence on the effects of aversive control allows at present of no simple summary, though there is perhaps a case for saying that, if in doubt, one should reinforce desired behaviour rather than punish undesired behaviour. Even, however, if the evidence were different the most that would follow would be that aversive control is sometimes a necessary evil, which is scarcely a controversial conclusion! To suppose that an operant psychologist is committed, without qualification, to preferring aversive kinds of control is clearly absurd.

(c) It is sometimes said that operant psychologists are too ready to inflict pain—including electric shock in particular—as part of their training programme. To be strict, such a criticism, if justified at all, would chiefly need to be directed against those who use the techniques of Pavlovian conditioning, such as aversion therapy, rather than against those who use operant techniques; the latter are concerned far more often with training by reward rather than training by punishment. In either case, however, the ethical issues are the same and relate to the use of pain in training and treatment.

We do not dispute that there can be moral dilemmas in this area, but they have no unique connections with the operant approach as such. In surgery and dentistry, for example, patients may sometimes suffer considerable pain; and while it is possible in logic that an individual may be at fault in permitting avoidable or unnecessary pain, there is clearly no justification for concluding that surgeons and dentists must from the nature of the case be inhumane people.

It may still be objected that those who undergo surgical or dental treatment have, whether explicitly or implicitly, given 'informed consent' to the treatment in question, and that, in contrast, operant techniques are sometimes used when no such consent has been given. Even if this is true, however (which is an empirical matter), it would not establish that there is necessarily anything inhumane about the use of operant techniques; it would show only that they can be misused, which is true also of surgical, dental, and most other techniques. We fully agree that, unless there are some very unusual circumstances, failure to obtain informed consent is ethically objectionable; and any attempt to use operant techniques in the absence of such consent would rightly merit the condemnatory term 'brain-washing'. There is no reason in logic, however, why the principle of 'informed consent' should not apply when treatment is based on operant principles just as much as it applies when treatment is of other kinds.

Ethical problems may, of course, arise if the person is too young or too ill to be capable of consenting in an informed way. In the case of a child it is widely agreed that consent by a parent or guardian is sufficient; but there may well be difficult decisions if an adult patient who is mentally ill refuses to agree to treatment which plainly will relieve him. There are, we believe, some particularly scrupulous psychiatrists who—at least in theory—would allow, say, a food-refusing schizophrenic patient to die rather than force-feed him. This seems to us mistaken, since it makes good sense to ask what the patient *would* have chosen had he not been ill; and if one is satisfied that in that case he would have accepted the treatment and that on his recovery he is likely to agree with what was done, then the use of force, even if this involves pain, cannot be regarded as objectionable, and indeed is surely what one would ask for in one's own case. Admittedly it is necessary to be satisfied that there are independent criteria of illness: one cannot conclude that a person is ill *merely* because he has decided not to eat, for instance, or because his ideas are eccentric or thought to be politically dangerous. This would be to argue in a circle. We do not dispute that in practice there may be all kinds of moral dilemmas as to the extent to which in a particular case one should apply pressure in trying to prevent a person from doing something to himself which in one's own opinion is harmful. We are suggesting only that problems about the use of such pressure are not peculiar to operant psychology and that an operant psychologist is in no way committed to preferring pressure to persuasion.

It may still be objected that when surgeons and dentists inflict pain they do so on the basis of a high degree of professional expertise and, at least in most cases, with full confidence that the outcome will be successful. Once again, however, there is no distinctive moral dilemma posed by the use of operant techniques. It is possible, certainly, that the operant psychologist may overestimate what he is capable of achieving, but this could be true of others also. Provided criteria for 'success' are agreed, then the probability of a successful outcome in a particular case is an empirical matter; and the principle of 'informed consent' implies that the patient has been told of this probability and can take into account possible loss in terms of pain, inconvenience, expense, and time in the likely or unlikely event of the treatment being unsuccessful.

(d) It has sometimes been a matter of concern to nurses and others that, under a regime of 'behaviour modification', they must no longer comfort patients who, for instance, cry or display temper trantrums but must reward only such behaviour as is socially desirable.

It does not seem to us that this matter should be blown up into a big issue. Common sense suggests that if a child is being difficult it may sometimes be preferable to ignore him rather than come rushing round with well-intentioned blandishments; and similarly it is surely worth reminding nurses that it is sometimes possible, even with the best of intentions, to reinforce undesirable behaviour. Obviously if they receive the idea that they should *never* comfort a child who cries or pay attention to someone displaying temper tantrums, they may well feel a conflict between their natural good sense and these new instructions. Clearly, however, it would be absurd in practice to specify in advance to all nurses what they should do in particular circumstances, and it is surely preferable that they should be taught to understand the concept of *reinforcement* and then be able to recognize what is needed in a particular case, rather than be given a set of invariable rules. It may also be helpful if they are trained to keep an accurate record of what happens, since when such records are examined a particular action, whether by themselves or the patient, may take on a new significance. On this particular issue there does not seem to us to be any ethical problem which cannot be solved by good sense and adequate communication of what operant techniques involve.

(e) There is an important difference between those situations where an experimental subject is aware of what schedule of reinforcement he is receiving and those situations where he is not. Similarly in ordinary life there is a difference between those situations where X knows what is Y's purpose in presenting particular stimuli and those where he has no such knowledge. Only in the latter case can any charge of 'trickery' be justified.

It has perhaps been a weakness of operant psychology in the past that these two kinds of situation have not been adequately distinguished. It is possible that some kind of misunderstanding of the conceptual position has been responsible for this: 'know' is a mentalistic concept, and if one assumes, with the methodological behaviourist, that what the person knows is irrelevant or undiscoverable, then, as a matter of logic, no distinction is possible between those situations which involve trickery and those which do not. Since, however, it is no part of the operant programme to deny the truth of particular sentences containing the word 'know', there can be no valid grounds on this score for disputing the importance of the distinction.

What we call 'training' can be redescribed in operant terms as presenting people with stimuli in such a way that their repertoire of possible responses becomes wider. In many cases such procedures are completely free from any kind of ethical objection. For example, a competent teacher or lecturer will present stimuli which he knows—or at least hopes—will result in specifiable responses (those which in ordinary speech would be called 'showing keenness' or 'showing understanding'). Not only do his audience expect such stimuli, but he would be less than competent if he did not attempt to present them in the most effective way possible. Ethical problems arise not from the presentation of stimuli whose consequences are known but from their presentation in a context where the recipient *does not himself know what is happening*. For example, it is possible that organizers of opinion polls may influence the voting behaviour of large numbers of people by publishing or failing to publish particular findings, while the people concerned are unaware that such influence is at work. In the same way it might be possible, by suitable arrangement of the contingencies, to persuade people to gamble or to buy a certain product without their being aware that someone is manipulating them; and there is an important difference between the situation where a person chooses to indulge in a 'flutter' with full knowledge of the risks or consciously decides to be influenced by a particular advertisement and the situation where he is the victim of pressures of which he is unaware. In so far as operant psychologists have failed to emphasize the difference between the two situations they have perhaps led people to think—quite erroneously—that operant techniques always involve manipulating people without their knowledge.

(f) Decisions as to what kinds of behaviour are desirable are not themselves part of operant psychology. To say this is, of course, to make a point of logic: in more precise terms, sentences which state what objectives are desirable are logically independent of sentences describing relationships between particular stimuli and particular responses. It follows that an operant psychologist with the requisite empirical knowledge is logically entitled to advise on *how to achieve* certain objectives but not—*qua* operant psychologist—to say what objectives should be aimed at.

In contrasting 'matters of fact' with 'matters of value' some philosophers have perhaps been guilty of oversimplification—particularly if they then assume an equivalence between the dichotomy into 'fact' and 'value' and the dichotomy into 'is' and 'ought', which can be seen on examination to be marking quite a different contrast. J. L. Austin's warning against 'the deeply ingrained worship of tidy-looking dichotomies' (1962, p. 3) is pertinent here. None the less, it seems to us important that practising psychologists should at least be aware of some of the logical distinctions which have been drawn by philosophers in this area. Only so can they avoid both the arrogance of seeming to tell other people what is good for them and the faint-heartedness of failing to claim expertise in circumstances where they are fully entitled to do so.

There may, of course, be plenty of situations in clinical psychology where no particular ethical dilemmas are involved. That a severely sub-normal child should be trained to feed himself and dress himself, that a person with a fear of spiders should be cured of such a fear, or that an alcoholic should cease to feel the craving for alcohol—these are objectives which will seldom in practice be matters of dispute. In such situations the task of the clinical psychologist is to find the most effective ways of bringing about a situation whose desirability is not in question. Where there is any doubt about objectives, however, or if an agreed objective can be brought about only at considerable risk or cost (e.g. in terms of adverse side-effects, uncertainty of success, or unavoidable pain), then he has a duty to discuss such matters fully with the patient or his relatives rather than provide them with what he himself thinks the patient needs. If one's child were likely to cease to display autistic behaviour as a result of a particular course of treatment, one would no doubt agree to the administration of quite severe electric shock, but one would certainly expect to be consulted in the first place and to have the chance to weigh the possible gains against the risks.

Decisions as to what is desirable are not, of course, completely beyond the reach of argument. Moral philosophers of an earlier generation sometimes said that we simply 'intuit' what is right or wrong, for example the wrongness of inflicting pain. If this was meant to imply, however, that rational communication on ethical issues is impossible it is mistaken. One can appeal to consistency, and one can point out some of the implications of a moral belief which another person may have overlooked. In addition one can appeal to 'coherence', in the sense that, for instance, a particular view as to what is desirable may cohere with a person's religious views about the world and man's place in it. All such issues are, however, logically independent of any specialist knowledge which one may have as an operant psychologist, and, as far as we know, an operant approach is compatible with a wide range of religious views.

Finally we should like to draw a comparison from the ethical point of view between therapy based on operant principles and therapy of a psychodynamic kind. We are in no way attacking the use of the latter, and, as we hope is plain from the tone of this book, we are opposed to sectarianism in general within psychology. None the less we should like to try to rectify a view which—so we suspect—is taken uncritically for granted in some quarters, even if not explicitly formulated. It is the view that the psychotherapist is a tender-minded individual who proceeds with 'loving concern' whereas the behaviour therapist is necessarily tough-minded and impersonal. The truth seems to us to be rather that both operant and psychodynamic techniques *can* be misused and that neither *need* be. If psychotherapy is the orthodox religion in some quarters we are tempted to point out with Lucretius (Book I, lines 82–83),

> . . . quod contra saepius illa
> Religio peperit scelerosa atque impia facta

If a child is schizophrenic, for instance, for biochemical reasons, it is surely downright cruelty to allow parents to believe that it is their fault that the tragedy has happened. Similarly, while 'humane' child-guidance workers may put on long faces and say that a child is 'emotionally disturbed' (a stimulus which is clearly 'punishing' for the parents), an operant orientation will lead such people to try to reinforce *constructive* behaviour on the part of the parents and to make positive remarks such as 'Since your child has this difficulty you will need to work twice as hard'. 'How has this child become schizophrenic?' is, on the operant approach, a less important question than 'How can we manipulate the environment so as to help him?'

We make this point not to decry psychotherapy but simply to correct the view that the operant approach is necessarily and invariably less humane.

3. It is important, at the outset, to recognize objections on conceptual grounds for what they are. As was made clear in Chapter 2, conceptual proposals can sometimes be wrong, but the grounds on which one judges them to be wrong need to be carefully considered. In particular, it needs to be remembered that if a given statement is true, no amount of conceptual revision can make it false. Skinner has aptly expressed the matter as follows:

> Keats drank confusion to Newton for analysing the rainbow, but the rainbow remained as beautiful as ever and became for many even more beautiful. Man has not changed because we look at him, talk about him, and analyse him scientifically. His achievements in science, government, religion, art and literature remain as they have always been, to be admired as one admires a storm at sea or autumn foliage or a mountain peak, quite apart from their origins and untouched by a scientific analysis. What does change is our chance of doing something. (Skinner, 1972, p. 213)

Sometimes the word 'behaviourism' is assumed to stand for a conception of human nature which does not do full justice to man's humanity. As has been made clear, however, our version of operant psychology is 'behaviourist' only in the sense that part of its programme requires that sentences containing words such as 'know' and 'recognize' require translation. Such translation does not involve a denial that there are characteristically human skills, nor are we disputing the obvious empirical truth that humans have better powers of recognition than, say, parrots. We have already shown in Chapters 5 and 6 why such translation is needed; and for present purposes it is sufficient to say that acceptance of such a programme—even if it were conceptually wrong, which we do not accept—would still not be inhumane or commit anyone to the view that humans and animals are no different. In passing it may be mentioned that we see no good grounds for using the expression 'stimulus–response psychology' as a way of adversely characterizing the operant approach. As far as operant psychology is concerned it makes sense to distinguish different kinds of stimuli from each other and different kinds of response from each other, but it makes no sense to suppose that anything could affect an organism other than a stimulus or that an organism could behave in any way other than emitting a response. Moreover an important point about operant concepts is precisely the fact that they are applicable universally: in *any* situation one can ask what the stimulus was and how the organism responded; one can ask what stimuli are likely to be reinforcing, what discriminative stimuli were present, and so on. To suppose that one might find entities other than stimuli and responses is like supposing that one might find a small section of a piece of music which was so beautiful that talk of amplitudes and frequencies was no longer appropriate. Indeed it is somewhat like supposing that those who insist that *all* music is describable in terms of amplitudes and frequencies are philistines who cannot appreciate beauty.

We fully agree that it is misleading to speak of 'operant *conditioning*', since the word 'conditioning' suggests purely mechanical responding without any weighing up of alternatives, and in point of fact the word 'conditioning' has largely disappeared from the operant literature. We also agree that the expression 'behaviour modification' as a description of what happens when operant techniques are used in a clinical setting is somewhat lacking in sensitivity. If the intention in using it is to stress the analogies with teaching and learning we can think of no good reason why the words 'teaching' and 'learning' should not themselves be used: no one need object to being taught something, but it is not unreasonable to react somewhat obstinately if it is suggested that one should have one's behaviour modified!

A possible objection to the operant conceptual scheme is that it makes psychologists too restrictive in their choice of topics for study. It might be suggested, for example, that operant psychologists have paid too little attention to loving and hating and indeed to the study of human relationships in general.

Now it is true, of course, as a matter of historical fact, that those with a psychodynamic orientation (e.g. Suttie, 1935; Bowlby, 1946) have been far more ready than so-called 'experimental' psychologists to call attention to loving and hating and to the importance of the human relations factor in general. Lorenz writes with warmth about his animals and birds, but if 'experimental' psychologists have felt any warmth toward their rats there is little evidence of this in their writings! Similarly those who have done research with human subjects in traditional experiments on perception and remembering, though they sometimes record whether or not the subjects were volunteers, seldom give any other detail which could be relevant to what the subjects *felt* about the tasks given to them.

Conceptually, however, there is no reason at all why operant psychologists should not direct their attention, more than they have in the past, towards loving and hating. These terms would of course need 'sharpening' if there is to be systematic research: one would need to specify at least a manageable range of responses which could appropriately count as being manifestations of love or hate. There is no reason in principle, however, why the variables affecting such responses should not be systematically studied, and the evidence adduced by Bowlby (1951) on the effects of maternal deprivation, though he himself would be the first to admit its shortcomings, is at least a first step in this direction. The main practical drawback to such research is that it is objectionable on ethical grounds deliberately to submit young children to maternal or any other kind of deprivation, and investigators must therefore perforce be content with correlational studies rather than operant studies in the strict sense. It would be very rash, however, to assert in advance that operant-type questions, such as 'What are the controlling variables?', are inappropriate in this or any other area. If the study of loving and hating has been neglected by operant psychologists in the past there is no theoretical reason why it should continue to be neglected in the future.

Some critics, too, may call attention to the total neglect on the part of operant psychologists of the phenomena of extra-sensory perception (ESP) and indeed of so-called 'paranormal' phenomena in general. Their refusal to look beyond the stimuli and responses of ordinary laboratory work would on this showing be additional evidence of their narrow-mindedness and cocksure dogmatism.

Now, as we see the situation, there is no logical reason why a person interested in such phenomena should not study them by means of operant techniques. What the results of such investigations would be is, of course, an empirical matter, and if positive results were regularly found this would justify continuing the investigation further. If operant psychologists have not so far worked in this field, this is presumably because they have not considered the phenomena to be of sufficient interest or importance. The onus, in our opinion, is on those who wish to promote such research to convince their scientific colleagues of the value of what they are doing. If, for example, an operant psychologist continually found that his experiments were being upset by the ability on the part of some subjects to say what was present in a stimulus display before it was presented (in a context where they were in no position to guess or infer this), it would be foolish—not just narrow-minded—to ignore such a phenomenon. One possible procedure might be to screen all subjects for ESP ability and exclude from any experiment on normal perception those believed to possess such ability, just as in some contexts one might choose to exclude colour-blind subjects from experiments which involved the distinguishing of different colours; alternatively one might decide that this phenomenon, like colour-blindness, was worth studying in its own right and select 'ESP-ability' subjects for special investigation.

If one turns to the main body of research literature in psychology, however, one finds that, outside journals devoted to ESP, no one ever reports having carried out either procedure.

It seems clear, therefore, that whatever they *profess* to believe about ESP, psychologists in their daily practice do not take it into account; and although professions of open-mindedness are commonly regarded as commendable, we regard it as dishonest and muddle-headed to claim to be open-minded, either on this issue or on any other, if one fails to put such professed open-mindedness into practice.

At this point it may be helpful to draw a distinction between so-called 'spontaneous' phenomena and the results of systematic experiment. An example of a 'spontaneous' phenomenon would be the case cited by McCreery (1967) in which, at the end of the First World War, a Royal Air Force pilot named McConnel was apparently 'seen' by a fellow officer named Larkin in their shared room at almost the very time when his plane was in fact crashing. In contrast, a systematic experiment would be one in which, for example, a subject was required to say what card is being exposed or thought about by someone in another room when he had not been told and was in no position to observe or make inferences. Now in the case of 'spontaneous' phenomena, as Broad (1962, p. 9) in effect implies, the research scientist may well not be the best person to judge what in fact happened; the need is rather for someone with a legal training or at any rate someone who is experienced in assessing the credibility of witnesses. Similarly if it is claimed that a named individual can bend spoons by means of forces so far unknown to physics, it is premature to call in physicists until one is sure that the effects are not simply the result of clever conjuring; the person needed is a professional conjuror. Moreover, professions of belief in this or that 'spontaneous' phenomenon are not particularly profitable unless the phenomenon in question can be fitted into some more comprehensive picture. Thus, if anyone were to say to us, the authors, 'What do *you* think happened in the McConnel case?', our answer would in fact be 'We have not the least idea.' Even, however, if we were to say something more positive such as 'The evidence seems fairly convincing', this would still give the research worker no indication what to look for next. Even in the case of experimental findings there is the same difficulty at least as far as past research is concerned. Thus it is reported by Soal and Bateman (1954) that two subjects, Basil Shackleton and Gloria Stewart, were consistently able to score 'better than chance' in card-guessing experiments over a long period. If, however, one is asked what one thinks happened, it is difficult to see how any answer could be more than a matter of opinion.

If an operant psychologist were to decide that card-guessing phenomena were worth study he would attempt in the first place to isolate the relevant controlling variables, and rather than run the same experiment over and over again he would systematically vary the conditions. Also he would insist, at least until some firm conclusions were established, on a conceptual scheme with minimal theoretical commitment. For this reason he would avoid phrases such as 'communication between minds', preferring instead simply to record the number of 'hits' and 'misses'. The analogies with 'perception' are in any case questionable, and if such alleged 'perception' is then described as 'extra-sensory' it is hard to see that this is anything more than a way of saying that ordinary sensory cues were not present. To eliminate the concept of *extra-sensory perception* is not, of course, to deny that certain individuals may in the future score 'better than chance' in card-guessing experiments; whether they will do so or not is an empirical matter. If, however, one uses a conceptual scheme which is relatively free from theoretical commitment one may be less inclined to theorize inappropriately about the results.

Indeed the basic difficulty in taking so-called 'ESP' research seriously is not an empirical one (for different people may hold different judgements of what is likely) but a conceptual one. People have supposed that if the results prove 'positive' this means that there are forces in the world hitherto undetected by physicists, that our ideas of space and time may have to be revised, that 'materialism' is finally refuted, and so on. As a matter of logic no such conclusions would follow. One would be entitled to say that certain people possessed a hitherto unsuspected kind of ability, and one might decide that this was something which was worth following up. The case, however, for talking about such phenomena in terms of 'extra-sensory perception' or for describing them as 'paranormal' would still not have been made out.

There is a further conceptual weakness in the case for ESP as it is commonly presented. In every other area of science one is looking for explanations of what happens, whereas ESP phenomena are thought to be important precisely to the extent that one *fails* to find explanations for them. If study of ESP is a branch of science it is the only branch of science which thrives on *absence* of explanation. It is rational, certainly, to check that in card-guessing experiments the subject is not using cues whose influence one wishes to exclude, but to be satisfied that something is *not* happening would in the rest of science be regarded only as a first step, not as an end in itself.

Finally, it is perhaps worth pointing out the consequences if ESP were found to be a regular phenomenon. It is no exaggeration to say that almost all other experiments in psychology would be rendered invalid. For instance, if one had originally supposed that one was studying the effects of certain kinds of inter-ference on the memorizing of lists of words, one could not now exclude the possibility that these kinds of interference were not the relevant variable at all; it could be that subjects were telepathically 'reading' what the experimenter was thinking. If one then arranged it so that the experimenter did not in fact know what the correct answers were, as would seemingly be possible if the checking and recording were carried out mechanically, it would still be the case that a human observer would have to know the answers at some point; and even if *per impossible* this were not so, one would not have excluded the possibility of clairvoyant precognition by the subject of the information stored in the machine. None of these considerations disproves the possibility of telepathy, clairvoyance, or precognition; but if they do occur the consequences would be more far-reaching than many people have appreciated. If traditional psychological research is to be possible at all it would need to be restricted to those for whom tests of ESP ability had proved negative.

Our conclusion is that those who fail to take ESP seriously are not therefore being 'soulless' or narrow-minded. Whether Larkin genuinely saw McConnel (in some legitimate sense of 'see') is an empirical matter; similarly it is an empirical matter whether people do or do not score 'better than chance' in card-guessing experiments. There is no particular operant 'line' on empirical matters; and if one uses the word 'possible' in the somewhat curious philosophical sense in which events which figure in any empirical claim are said to be possible, then certainly in this sense ESP is a possibility. This does not mean, however, that one is committed to following advocates of ESP on the conceptual side; and, as we have indicated several times in this book, what seems at first sight to be commendable open-mindedness sometimes turns out on examination to be acquiescence in conceptual muddle.

Two final points on the conceptual side require mention. First, although many of the arguments which purport to show that operant psychology is 'soulless' seem to us invalid, there is one respect in which the operant conceptual scheme in its present form has, in our view, led to an imbalance. The cumulative record, for all its merits, is a device which encourages psychologists to place special emphasis on the question of *how often* particular responses occur. The frequency of a particular behavioural event, however, is not the only significant aspect of that event. For example, if a person is sitting still in a concert hall showing every sign of enjoying the music, it would be absurd to say that the only significant question which can be asked about such behaviour is, 'How often will it occur in the future?' Indeed, there are many significant events in human experience which happen only once in a lifetime, or at any rate too few times to justify anyone in taking a measure of frequency—birth, starting off at school or college, graduation, falling in love, getting married, having children, and, alas, dying! It seems that our present preoccupation with rate of 'easily repeatable' responses cannot embrace phenomena of this sort, and this is something which will clearly require attention in the future. Second, as we shall try to show in Chapter 12, there are grounds for saying that when human behaviour—as opposed to animal behaviour—is being studied a further concept is needed, viz. that of an *informative stimulus*. This concept therefore calls attention to certain important *differences* between human and animal responding. Operant psychology will not be made any more humane in allowing oneself to be hood-winked by words. The fact, however, that a distinctive concept is needed when the behaviour of human subjects is being studied may perhaps be a reassurance to those who might otherwise suppose that operant psychologists regard man as nothing more than a rather complicated kind of rat.

Chapter 9

Conceptual Problems in the Clinical Field

It is commonly supposed that if one takes the operant approach seriously one is thereby committed in the clinical field to favouring programmes of behaviour therapy rather than those of psychotherapy.

This seems to us to be an area where conceptual analysis is urgently called for. We are not suggesting that such analysis can resolve all outstanding controversies, but we hope at the very least to dispose of those disputes which are unnecessary and to make it easier for psychiatrists and clinical psychologists to consider empirical issues on their merits.

We shall argue that doctrinaire allegiance to one 'side' or the other is unhelpful and that (in so far as it is appropriate to talk of 'sides') each side has important contributions to make, both conceptually and empirically.

The terms 'behaviour therapy' and 'psychotherapy' both cover a wide range of different procedures, and it may even be that in the last resort the distinction between them lacks theoretical justification. Since it is a distinction which is widely used in practice, however, we shall make it our starting-point. As a rough indication of the difference between the two, one might say that behaviour therapy is concerned with removing the main presenting feature—enuresis or fear of snakes, for example—in accordance with principles explicitly derived from laboratory studies of learning, while psychotherapy is concerned with a re-orientation, to a greater or lesser degree, of the personality as a whole, the presenting feature being regarded merely as a symptom of something more important. In practice this has meant that in psychotherapy the patient is encouraged to talk not only about his present feelings (both towards the therapist and towards others) but about experiences in the past which appear to have been significant for him, whereas in behaviour therapy the patient's feelings towards the therapist are not usually regarded as relevant nor are inferences commonly made as to what might be the 'meaning' of a presenting feature. In addition, psychotherapists sometimes argue that if one treats the presenting feature in isolation then 'symptom substitution' is likely to occur; for example, if as a result of behaviour therapy a child ceases to be enuretic but undergoes no basic change in personality or life-style, then some other antisocial behaviour, such as truancy from school, can often be expected.

Now it might seem at first glance that questions about the effectiveness of different types of therapy are empirical ones, and on this showing any disagreement which exists is due to the complexity of the facts and the difficulty of presenting findings in such a way that valid conclusions can be drawn. Reflection suggests, however, that the word 'effectiveness' itself gives rise to conceptual problems; and in particular it may be that a psychotherapist might wish in some contexts to insist on more stringent criteria of effectiveness than would a behaviour therapist. He might point out, for instance, that a person's answers to a personality questionnaire provide no firm basis for judging whether or not he has responded to treatment, and even evidence of greater happiness at work or the easing of family tensions may from a psychodynamic point of view be less than satisfactory. It is important in this connection not to overlook the fact that valid judgements can often be made on the basis of the clinical 'feel' of a case; and there seems little doubt that skilled psychotherapists are sometimes able to make use of a variety of small cues about which they may not even be fully articulate. An appeal to such clinical judgements may not convince the sceptical, and in the wrong hands there is the possibility of abuse. In our opinion, however, the value of these judgements has been underrated by psychologists, particularly by those who press on all occasions for statistical surveys: a clinical judgement does not profess to be anything more than it is, whereas statistical surveys can sometimes create the illusion of valid knowledge when in fact wholly inappropriate questions have been asked. Where investigators disagree over criteria for 'effectiveness' there is perhaps a prima facie case for preferring those criteria which seem the most sensitive: thus a verbal report from a patient that he is 'getting on all right', though by no means a negligible piece of evidence if sincerely given, affords a relatively insensitive criterion of effectiveness of treatment in comparison, for example, with responses which in some way indicate that he has 'come to terms with himself'.

It follows from all this that discussions as to whether this or that procedure is effective are liable to be unprofitable unless agreed criteria are laid down for what is to count as 'effectiveness'. It may even be that different procedures have different objectives; and in that case it would be perfectly sensible for a behaviour therapist and a psychotherapist to work together as members of a team, discussion taking place between both of them and the patient as to what kind of objective is to be aimed at.

There are related conceptual problems over the notion of *symptom substitution*. Thus it is clearly not enough to regard *any* mishap which occurs after, say, the enuresis has cleared up as a case of symptom substitution; there must be grounds of some kind for supposing that the events are connected. Indeed, it is precisely because many events *could be* examples of symptom substitution that it is difficult to assert with confidence that a particular event actually *is* one. If a child who has ceased to be enuretic soon afterwards breaks his leg the conclusion that he is 'producing a substitute symptom' is justified only if there is evidence for a coherent pattern of behaviour of which breaking a leg might form a part. One would not expect the psychotherapist to predict the exact form which the production of a substitute symptom would take, but the less he excludes from his prediction the less convincing his claim becomes that substitute symptoms occur at all. Basically what is at issue is the truth of an unfulfilled hypothetical statement; to say that the child's breaking his leg is a substitute symptom is to assert that it would not have occurred had the child continued to be enuretic. This is, of course, an empirical matter, though because one is discussing what would have happened if something else had been different there can in principle be no discovery which would settle the matter definitively.

Once criteria for 'effectiveness' are agreed, of course, then questions about the relative effectiveness of different procedures are empirical ones; and, similarly, provided agreement can be reached over what is to count as 'symptom substitution', then the question whether or how often symptom substitution occurs is also an empirical one.

There remains, however, a more basic source of conflict which would not necessarily be resolved even if there were no disagreement over empirical matters. What is at issue, we suggest, is a dispute between the two sides as to the appropriate conceptual scheme or 'model'. There are, of course, many different kinds of model, in this sense, which explictly or implicitly are used in clinical work. Thus Siegler and Osmond (1966), in a discussion limited to schizophrenia only, distinguish no less than six such models (and to distinguish even this number is regarded by them as something of an oversimplification). Each of these models, on their view, serves to 'raise a set of questions about what sort of a thing schizophrenia is, what should be done about it, and how the people involved ought to behave' (p. 1193). They also point out in a very interesting way how an implicit choice of concepts may affect clinical practice. 'Most programmes', they say, 'unknowlingly involve two or more theories which, if seriously and consistently applied, would have diverse and mutually incompatible consequences. . . In a laboratory study such confusion would be merely unworkable; in the daily care of schizophrenic patients it is likely to be disastrous' (Siegler and Osmond, 1966).

At the risk of oversimplifying, however, we shall limit ourselves, for purposes of the present argument, to a two-fold classification: we shall speak of the 'medical' model and the 'behavioural' model. Even choice of descriptive labels is somewhat difficult here, and it is not the case that all doctors use the one model and all behavioural scientists the other. What is being distinguished, however, will, we hope, be sufficiently clear in the discussion which follows.

One possibility, then, is to take a *medical* approach to clinical work. On this showing the person whom a clinician meets professionally is a *patient*; he is *ill*; his condition is *diagnosed*; he requires *treatment*, and may in some cases need to be treated in a *hospital*. It is important, too, that the diagnosis should get at the root *cause* of his symptoms; to treat the symptoms on their own is at best a palliative and may even divert attention away from providing long-term help. If treatment is successful the patient is said to be *cured*.

Those who support a programme of behaviour therapy have in effect argued that the medical model is inadequate—inadequate, that is, in the sense that it leads people to misinterpret or misunderstand what they are doing and may even encourage them to do the wrong things. What they are offering can thus be regarded as a set of proposals for redescription: in these proposals the words 'patient', 'ill', 'diagnosis', 'treatment' and 'cure' either disappear altogether or are used, like 'sunrise', because it is labour-saving to make do with conventional words. The person whom they are trying to help is in important respects like the subject of a psychological experiment, and even if for convenience he is termed a 'patient' this does not mean that he is ill in any standard sense: one should think rather in terms of maladaptive behaviour, since the affinities are with teaching and learning rather than with dosing, dissecting, or prescribing diets. It is a similar reluctance to speak of 'patients' which had led psychiatric social workers to use the word 'client', though, as Wootton (1959, Chapter 8) has aptly pointed out, this word begs a number of questions as to what the role of a psychiatric social worker should be. Similarly there is not much occasion in behaviour therapy to use the word 'diagnosis'. To diagnose is to assign a label, and, since these labels are usually nouns, the argument here is that there is some risk that one may be diverted from studying what is important, viz. how the subject behaves. To say that someone suffers from condition A is on this showing to say that he is likely to emit A-like behaviour, and though a particular label may give some indication as to what behaviour to expect it is misleading to ascribe any kind of ontological status to condition A over and above its manifestations in behaviour. Finally, there are logical grounds, on this approach, for hesitation over use of the word 'cure'. The point of importance, it would be said, is that the 'patient', having formerly behaved in certain ways, now no longer does so; whether he has been 'cured' in any further sense does not arise. To put the matter epigrammatically, if one uses the word 'illness' at all, then from the behavioural point of view the symptoms *are* the illness, while if one uses the word 'cure' the disappearance of the symptoms *is* the cure.

Does it follow, then, that 'X suffers from condition A' is simply another way of saying that X is manifesting A-like symptoms? Such a thesis, we suggest, can be made true only at the cost of trivialization. This can be shown as follows. In the ordinary way the notion of a symptom is parasitic upon the notion of an underlying cause, and in many branches of medicine it is helpful to distinguish symptoms (increased body temperature, increased intake of fluid, the presence of a rash, or whatever it may be) from underlying causes such as vitamin deficiency or the action of identifiable germs. In these cases one could defend the thesis that 'the symptoms *are* the illness' by saying that the absence of the vitamins or the action of the germs are *further symptoms*. This, however, is to make a trivial point, since having made it, one would still need to distinguish those symptoms which were from those other being immediately manifested 'symptoms' which were formerly called the underlying cause.

A more helpful distinction, it seems to us (though once again we are no doubt oversimplifying), is between those medical terms which are 'nosographic' and those which are 'nosologic'. This distinction is referred to by Hermann (1959) and can be explained as follows: a nosographic concept is one which describes the course of an illness but makes no claim about underlying causes; a nosologic concept is one which both describes the course of an illness and entails certain views as to its origin. Thus in the present state of knowledge *fever* is a nosographic concept while *tuberculosis* is a nosologic one. In the former case, if the patient looked flushed and had a high temperature it would be logically impossible to deny that he was feverish; in the latter case, even if it were true that there was coughing and blood in the sputum one would not say that it was a genuine case of tuberculosis unless a causal explanation in terms of the action of identifiable bacilli was found to be correct. As knowledge advances, of course, a concept may cease to be merely a nosographic one and acquire the status of a nosologic one.

In the light of this distinction it is now possible to restate the behaviour therapist's claim in a more convincing way. There is no need for him to insist that 'the symptoms *are* the illness' is true throughout the whole of medicine; his argument requires only that it should be true in the case of nosographic concepts. When these are used there can by definition be no grounds other than the presence of identifiable symptoms for saying that a particular condition or illness is present; and 'curing' this condition or illness cannot therefore mean anything more than removing the symptoms. Indeed the word 'symptom' itself, from the behaviour therapist's point of view, is in part misleading, since the implied polar term is 'underlying cause'. More strictly, his point is that we should speak of 'maladaptive behaviour' and leave out altogether any reference to symptoms or causes.

The next move in the behaviour therapist's argument is crucial. Psychiatry, he would say, is in many respects not as far advanced as other branches of medicine; and if we examine familiar clinical concepts such as *phobia* or *depression*, it becomes obvious that they are nosographic in character. In these cases what we know is that the patient is *behaving* in certain ways, for example by exhibiting irrational fears or showing signs of unhappiness or self-depreciation in an inappropriate context, and we know very little about any events inside his body which may be causing such behaviour. It is therefore a perfectly reasonable objective to help him to behave differently; if we do so this is all the 'curing' which is logically possible.

Those who describe their therapy in 'psychodynamic' terms have, on this view, misled themselves. They have assumed that clinical concepts are nosologic and have therefore made the 'medical'-type assumption that one should treat causes and not symptoms. Since no ordinary causes have been discovered, such as biochemical abnormalities, they have had recourse to mythological causes such as 'conflicts of forces within the psyche', and it is these forces which they have supposed to be in need of realignment. This mythology has led them into believing that even when manifest symptoms have been removed substitute symptoms will reappear. They are therefore guilty of taking as an incontrovertible empirical fact what is only the logical consequence of certain misleading features of their conceptual scheme.

Even, however, if the psychotherapist acknowledges the force of these conceptual points, he is not necessarily committed to any change in his current practice. This can be shown as follows. Let us suppose that the question is one of how best to help someone who says that he is troubled by an irrational fear of spiders. In such a case, if the person decided, after rational discussion, that he simply wanted to be rid of this fear and was not seeking treatment with any other relevant objective, conscious or otherwise, then some form of behaviour therapy would seem to be appropriate. An experienced psychotherapist, however, as a result of his orientation, might be inclined to ask what such a fear 'meant' in the life of the patient: he would regard it as a 'presenting symptom' whose origin might be traced to painful experiences at an earlier time in the patient's life. If, therefore, the patient agreed, again after suitable discussion, that his fear of spiders was a manifestation of some underlying personal insecurity, then there would be a case for advising psychotherapy. Now it is important to recognize that *there is no way of deciding between these two policies on conceptual grounds.* If a particular kind of unwanted behaviour occurs, such as displays of fear in the presence of spiders, it is an empirical matter whether one is justified in inferring the likelihood of other kinds of unwanted behaviour; and it is an empirical matter, too, whether unwanted behaviour of any kind can be removed more effectively by, say, the techniques of desensitization than by encouraging the patient to talk about things which happened to him earlier in life. Not least, it is an empirical matter whether discussion of the patient's feelings towards the therapist is one of the factors which contributes to the desired objective. From the conceptual point that statements about a person's feelings require translation it does not follow that such feelings are unimportant, and the fact that statements containing the word 'meaning' and the words 'inner life' give rise to problems of conceptual analysis does not establish that one should never ask what an action on the part of the patient means or assume that his inner life is unimportant. The procedures associated with psychotherapy can quite well be described in operant terms, and disagreements about how these procedures should be characterised need to be distinguished from disagreements over empirical matters.

If this argument is right, there are no grounds in operant psychology for any doctrinaire or *a priori* belief in the effectiveness of behaviour therapy; what procedures are effective (provided there is agreement about objectives) is an empirical matter.

In addition, once it is clear that part of the controversy between behaviour therapists and psychotherapists is conceptual in character, one can examine the advantages and disadvantages of particular ways of talking without feeling that the commitment to one conceptual scheme or the other is overriding. The advantages of the analogy with learning seem to us so obvious as to be beyond dispute. Equally, however, one is made aware from a consideration of psycho-dynamic concepts that it may not always be wise policy to take the presenting feature at its face value; and, even more important, one is alerted to the fact that in some circumstances the personality of the therapist may be one of the controlling variables. Once again it is a case 'say what you like', though it needs to be emphasized that in the clinical field the reasons both for and against the adoption of a particular conceptual model will probably be very complex, and in our opinion it is therefore very desirable to train clinical psychologists to be 'multilingual'. The situation seems to us to be admirably summed up in the following passage written by Skinner:

> A conception of human behaviour based primarily on clinical information and practice will undoubtedly differ from a conception emanating from the laboratory. This does not mean that either is superior to the other, or that eventually a common formulation will not prove useful to both . . . As psychiatry moves more rapidly into experimental research and as laboratory results take on a greater clinical significance, certain problems in the analysis of behaviour should become common to researcher and therapist alike, and should eventually be given common and cooperative solutions. (Skinner, 1969, p. 260)

Chapter 10

The Concept of *Control*

One of the key concepts in Skinner's *Science and Human Behaviour* (Skinner, 1953) is that of *control*. Thus he speaks of the control exercised by society through, for instance, political and religious institutions and of the possibility of diversifying the controlling agencies and limiting their power. In *Verbal Behaviour* (Skinner, 1957) he shows how it is possible to examine the variables which control what people say as well as those which control what they do. His basic argument is that, as science advances, knowledge of the variables which influence human behaviour will gradually increase. Since such knowledge gives the possibility of control, it is preferable, on his view, that such control should be rationally planned rather than left to chance or permitted as a result of inertia to pass into the hands of the unscrupulous.

Some people—Chomsky and Koestler, for instance—appear to find Skinner's ideas uncongenial, and there are even those who say that they find them frightening. Although it is likely that there have been misunderstandings of a more general kind as to what Skinner is claiming, an important source of the apparent dispute seems to be a group of unresolved problems connected with the concept of *control*. We shall argue in what follows that in Skinner's hands this concept has undergone a shift of meaning—one which is undoubtedly exciting, albeit potentially misleading for the unwary. In our view an operant psychologist must perforce take the concept of *control* seriously, but it does not follow that he is committed either to any extravagant philosophical claims (e.g. the belief that there is no such thing as free will) or to any questionable political or educational ideas (e.g. the belief that there should be more restrictions on personal freedom). We shall argue that those whose job it is to search for controlling variables are not logically required to be in favour of an increased amount of social control, since the word 'control' in these two expressions is not being used in the same sense.

In many of the original operant experiments the experimenters were successful in training animals to respond in certain ways, and in situations such as these it is clearly appropriate to say that the experimenter is controlling the animal's behaviour. Directly we start to extrapolate to human subjects, however, the conceptual issues become more complex. Although differences between humans and animals may seemingly be emphasized or played down according to the conceptual scheme which one adopts, in the last resort, as we have pointed out already, the extent of these differences is an empirical matter. Since in traditional operant psychology, however, there is the same basic method—that of recording the frequency of particular responses over a period of time—whatever species the experimenter has chosen to study, and since the concept of *control* is clearly applicable when animal subjects are involved, it appears to follow that it must be applicable to humans no less than to animals. Moreover, since there has clearly been success in predicting both human and animal behaviour, it seems not unreasonable to look forward to the time when *all* such behaviour is predictable; and the suggestion that there may be some actions—perhaps human ones in particular—which will never be brought under stimulus control would on this showing be both rash and obscurantist.

It is tempting to say, therefore, that all behaviour, including human behaviour, is under the control of prior stimuli and that in the last resort no action is ever capricious. The idea that some actions are 'free' is therefore illusory, since even apparently free actions will turn out ultimately to have been controlled, and similarly it seems impossible that any action should ever be spontaneous if this means 'occurring without the operation of prior controlling stimuli'.

There is a further complication. It is widely agreed that if a person is not free to choose a particular act it would be wrong to hold him responsible for it; and if belief in freedom is to be abandoned it seems to follow that belief in responsibility should be abandoned also. Similarly, on this showing, it appears that on an operant approach there can be no legitimate grounds for admiring people or praising them nor for regarding them as evil or blaming them.

These are alarming and paradoxical conclusions. In what follows we shall try to trace them to their source, and we shall argue that it is possible to retain the insights while avoiding the paradox. The basic mistake—and even Skinner has in our opinion misled himself on this matter—is to fail to look at the key words in the language-game which is their original home. To quote Berkeley (*Third Dialogue between Hylas and Philonous*): 'There is cause to suspect several erroneous conceits of the philosophers are owing to the same original: . . . they began to build their schemes, not so much on notions as words, which were framed by the vulgar, merely for conveniency and dispatch in the common actions of life, without any regard to speculation.' In our view, 'free', 'capricious', and 'spontaneous' are just such words.

Our next task must therefore be to consider whether these startling conclusions about freedom are justified or whether some logical error has crept in. For this purpose we shall examine the passage in *Verbal Behaviour* (Skinner, 1957, pp. 253–254) where Skinner indicates that a person's utterance of the word 'pencil' is an example of the control of verbal behaviour by prior stimuli. In this passage Skinner writes:

> Suppose we accept the engineering task of evoking a given response in a given speaker at a given time. To make the result important, let us suppose that a fairly large wager has been made: an English-speaking subject,

unaware of the point of the experiment, is to be made to emit a common response, say, *pencil*. If we are reasonably free to arrange external circumstances as we please, what should we do? Obviously the quickest way to win would be to mand the response by saying to the subject *Please say 'pencil'*. The history of most English-speaking people with respect to such a verbal stimulus would almost certainly produce the desired result. But if this step has been ruled out, we shall have to introduce other variables characteristic of other operants having the same form of response. If the wager is a sizeable one, we shall probably introduce many of these at once in order to raise the probability of the response to the maximum.

To strengthen a mand of this form we could make sure that no pencil or writing instrument is available, then hand our subject a pad of paper appropriate to pencil sketching, and offer him a handsome reward for a recognizable picture of a cat. We have not 'created the need for a pencil' in the sense of generating a state of deprivation, but we have strengthened behavior which can be executed only with a pencil. Under similar conditions the response *pencil* has frequently been reinforced and hence will become more probable.

One's first reaction to the above passage may perhaps be a certain feeling of anticlimax. One might assume from the context—particularly when a wager is said to be involved—that the person is to be *tricked* into saying the word 'pencil'. There is nothing in Skinner's description, however, to suggest that the person was not responding perfectly freely. If someone had said to him, 'Say the word "pencil" or I will shoot you' this would, of course, have been quite a different matter. As things are, what is promised or expected sounds alarming; what is given is—from the ethical point of view—entirely harmless.

We may note in passing that Skinner speaks of evoking the response 'pencil' as a task in *engineering*. This is in line with his view that the operant psychologist who works in the applied field is a 'behavioural engineer'. The analogy is presumably with tasks in electrical or mechanical engineering, where a consumer specifies the required end-product while the engineer himself uses his expertise to bring about what is requested of him. To say that an operant psychologist is a kind of engineer is not necessarily a blunder, but it is certainly a challenging conceptual innovation!

Now it has not always been noticed that when Skinner uses the word 'control' a subtle shift of meaning sometimes takes place. In his usage, if X and Y talk to each other and each is influenced in his responses by what the other says, then each is controlling the other. In this sense, too, an experimenter may be controlled by the behaviour of his subjects, since what he does in the next experiment is almost always affected by his subjects' behaviour in the previous one. There is a well-known cartoon in which one rat is depicted as saying to another, 'Gee, have I got this guy conditioned! Every time I press the lever he gives me a pellet.' Despite the apparent paradox, it is perfectly valid to say that in this sense of the word 'control' rats sometimes control the behaviour of humans. If it is pointed out that the experimenter knows what is happening whereas the rat does not, it is worth replying that even familiar uses of 'control' do not necessarily imply *conscious* control: thus a master switch may control the power supply to a house, and in psychodynamic thinking it is a commonplace that one person should control another's behaviour without realizing it.

When we say that a new sense of the word 'control' is involved we do not of course mean that the old and new senses are entirely unrelated. Skinner's intention is undoubtedly to exhibit the similarities between those situations where a rat's behaviour is controlled (in the straightforward sense) by the experimenter and those situations where a person's behaviour is 'controlled' (in inverted commas) in the sense of being the outcome of present and past events in his environment. Use of the word 'control' in both cases is a startling and exciting way of emphasizing this important similarity. It is as though Skinner said, 'If I say, "What is this?" and you say, "A pencil", this, too, is a case of control; and if sometimes we control ineffectively this is likely to be because our knowledge is inadequate.' He would, of course, agree that a redescription involving the use of the word 'control' does not make the facts any different from what they were (cf. Skinner, 1972, p. 213), but his intention is to exhibit the similarities between the control exerted in laboratory experimentation and the 'control' which each of us exerts in social situations. Moreover he is clearly correct in implying that there is nothing immoral about trying to change people's habits of verbal behaviour. 'Stating the matter in the most selfish light', he writes, 'I have been trying to get the reader to behave verbally as I behave. What teacher, writer, or friend does not?' (1957, p. 455).

Now we do not dispute that this proposal—as it is in effect—for an extended use of the concept of *control* is informative and exciting. It is a matter, however, of common experience among philosophers that conceptual proposals in one area tend to affect the surrounding territory. In particular, what is in fact no more than a logical consequence of a particular conceptual proposal tends to be mistaken for a fresh empirical truth. In this case one is immediately inclined to say that *all* behaviour is under the control of prior stimuli. This thesis is tempting because even if in practice one cannot isolate all the controlling variables one still wants to insist that such isolation is possible in principle. None the less it is also misleading. This is primarily because there is no polar opposite to be excluded. 'All behaviour is under the control of prior stimuli' sounds like an empirical claim, and the notion of 'all' is parasitic upon the possibility that *some* behaviour might not be under such control. If the argument is sound, however, this is no genuine possibility at all: as a matter of logic there can be no use for the expression, 'This behaviour was not under the control of any prior stimuli', and if apparently such behaviour occurs one does not say that there were no controlling stimuli; one says that the controlling stimuli are as yet unknown. 'All behaviour is under the control of prior stimuli' is thus a fraudulent statement: it masquerades as something exciting and provocative, but it would carry weight only if a genuine contrast was involved and one which allowed of empirical refutation.

It is also tempting, and again misleading, to say that no behaviour is ever capricious and that no behaviour is ever free. 'If we knew enough', it might be suggested, 'we should recognize that behaviour does not just occur capriciously. Any behaviour will be found, in the last resort, to be a function of the preceding stimuli.' It is this kind of consideration which leads Skinner to deliver his interesting—but in our opinion misguided—attack on 'autonomous man', a being who is assumed to act altogether independently of previous stimuli. Skinner's argument is that the area left under the control of 'autonomous man' recedes as a science of behaviour advances, and since on empirical grounds he believes that advances are continually being made the end result must necessarily be the demise of autonomous man and the denial of 'free will as an inner causal agent' (1953, p. 116). 'The hypothesis that man is not free', he writes (1953, p. 447), 'is essential to the application of scientific method to the study of behaviour.'

At best, however, Skinner has made his point in a misleading way. To imply, as he regularly does, that as a science of behaviour advances the control 'shifts' from autonomous man to the environment seems to suggest the substitution of one controlling agency for another. It of course makes sense to speak of stimuli in the environment causing particular responses, but it is clear on reflection that there is no use for the expression 'X himself was the cause of his own behaviour' (cf. Urmson, 1952, p. 191), and to use language which implies that 'autonomous man' and 'the environment' are alternative causal explanations of what people do suggests that it is an empirical matter that the former is gradually losing control, which clearly it is not.

Similarly it is an empirical matter whether telling people to 'try harder' or exert 'will power' is an effective way of changing their behaviour. The danger here is that faulty conceptual analysis may lead to the view that such exhortations are appeals to autonomous man to exert some kind of non-material 'heave' against the controlling variables in the environment (with the implication that a person's actions are of moral worth only if such 'heaves' are successful). This mythology is unnecessary: there are plenty of familiar grounds for saying whether or not someone is trying hard, while the expression 'will power' is regularly used when people display determination in adverse circumstances. All such conceptual trouble can be avoided by a consideration of the way in which the relevant words are used in the language-game which is their original home.

It is curious, too, that Skinner refers to the claim 'Man is not free' as a *hypothesis*. A hypothesis is something which is capable in principle of being refuted, whereas if a research worker failed in a particular case to discover what were the variables controlling a person's behaviour this would do nothing to strengthen the alternative hypothesis that in some cases people are free. The essential characteristic of a hypothesis is therefore being disallowed.

Moreover, even if 'presupposition' were substituted for 'hypothesis' there is still the danger of being misled. This can be shown if one asks what are the polar terms to 'capricious' and 'free' and what is therefore being excluded. Here, too, we need to ask how these words are used in the language-game which is their original home. Thus a parent or a teacher would be said to be behaving capriciously if what he did was inconsistent: it would be capricious, for instance, to cane a child on one occasion when he had done nothing wrong and take no action on another occasion despite some serious misdemeanour. It is perhaps helpful, again after the manner of Wittgenstein, to consider a particular individual and ask if *he* ever acts capriciously. Whether he does so or not is an empirical question, and it is certainly odd to claim (or appear to be claiming) that neither he nor anyone else *ever* does so.

Similarly in the case of the word 'free' one needs to bear in mind, following Austin, that it is the word 'unfree' which can be said to 'wear the trousers' (Austin, 1962, p. 15. If we say that a person is free this can in some contexts mean simply that he has no prior engagement; in other contexts it could mean that he is no longer in prison or no longer tied up. The constraints which can be imposed on someone so as to make him 'unfree' are of many different kinds, and Austin suggests that philosophers sometimes make the mistake of asking if a person is free (or, indeed, if people in general are free) without specifying the context.

In general, use of the word 'capricious' is parasitic on the possibility of some actions not being capricious and use of the word 'free' is parasitic on the possibility of some actions not being free. In discussing this problem Skinner seems to us to have failed to notice this crucial conceptual point.

One might perhaps re-frame his thesis by saying that in a fully developed science of behaviour there would be no need for the distinction between *capricious* and *not capricious* nor for the distinction between *free* and *not free*. There is no problem, on this view, as to how a person could have learned to use these words, since we have all met plenty of situations where we did not have adequate knowledge of the controlling variables, and the distinction between these situations and those where we do have such knowledge is clearly a valid one. The argument still does not establish, however, that no action is ever capricious or ever free in the standard sense of the words; it establishes only that sometimes we know what are the controlling variables and that sometimes we do not.

The truth seems to be that, over the word 'free' in particular, Skinner sometimes lapses into what may be called a 'pre-Rylean' position: 'free', it seems, means 'under the control of autonomous man' much as the mentalistic words discussed by Ryle (1949) are assumed— on the view which he is attacking—to refer to episodes in the life of a 'ghost' who is 'non-material', 'non-physical', or made of 'not-clockwork'. Provided freedom in the familiar sense is preserved, however, none of us need be worried at the prospect of losing our freedom in this pre-Rylean sense. 'A piece of sensible bread', says Philonous to Hylas in Berkeley's *Third Dialogue*, '. . . would stay my stomach better than ten thousand times as much of that insensible, unintelligible, real bread you speak of'; and similarly none of us will be worse off if we are deprived of 'real' freedom in some misconceived philosophical sense. The correct account, of course, is that an act is free if there is no coercive control, and indeed at times Skinner comes near to saying this (cf. 1972, Chapter 2). Had he done so, his view would have been very close to that of Austin, whose argument, as we have seen, is that what prevents a person from being free may be different in different circumstances.

Similar arguments apply over the word 'capricious'. An act is capricious if the agent follows no rational principle; and it is an obvious empirical truth that at times some people act capriciously while at times they do not. In either case, of course, it would be possible to look for the controlling variables; and in a particular case one might discover, for instance, that a person acted capriciously only under certain kinds of stress.

The same point can be exhibited further by consideration of the so-called 'smiling bridegroom' argument, as discussed by Flew (1966) and others. To say of a young man that he is marrying a girl of his own free choice implies, for instance, that he was not browbeaten into marrying her by his father. The example is cited in the philosophical literature as a paradigm case of a free action, and it is argued that one can reply to the sceptic by saying, 'If such an action was not freely chosen then I do not know what "freely chosen" means.' The important point is this: just because one may in the long run be able to discover all the controlling variables of which particular responses are a function, no consequences follow about the presence or absence of coercive control and therefore no consequences as to whether the action was or was not free.

One can admittedly conceive of situations in which people believed that they were acting freely when in fact they were not doing so. The behaviour of a person responding to post-hypnotic suggestion is an example; and if many human actions turned out to involve the same sort of thing, viz. unwitting obedience in doing what someone else has suggested, this would indeed be alarming, since one would have empirical grounds for saying that apparently free actions were not really free at all. Similarly if a person were *told* that he would say the word 'pencil' (a condition which Skinner specifically excludes in his discussion) and, despite all efforts to hold himself back, found that he was doing so, or if he were confronted with a series of prophecies which one by one were fulfilled despite his efforts to circumvent them, this too would be alarming; indeed he might well have the feeling that some hideous fate was hanging over him. As things are, however, there is good reason for believing that a person who is told, for instance, that he will shortly say the word 'pencil' will almost always be able to please himself whether he actually does so. Information that his friends had been laying wagers as to whether or not he will say the word might be expected to act as one of the controlling variables, as also might his past experience of the people making the wager (since he might prefer one rather than the other to win). From these considerations, however, it in no way follows that he is being *made* or *compelled* to say the word 'pencil', and whether he said the word freely or under compulsion is quite a different issue.

The argument that in a science of behaviour there is no room for praise or blame seems to us similarly fallacious. Ryle (1949, p. 80) sums up the mistake in a single sentence: he speaks of the 'silly view' which 'assumes that an action could not merit favourable or unfavourable criticism, unless it were an exception to scientific generalisations'. It might be possible, for example, in a science of behaviour, to know all the conditions in which a particular subject, X, manifested kindly behaviour towards children, and on this basis one could predict when such kindly behaviour was likely to occur; but one is not thereby logically prevented from admiring such kindness. Similarly if Y shows predictable cruelty the fact that it was predictable does not make him the less to blame. Indeed it is often the unpredictable events which one tends to excuse. Thus if a particular piece of apparent cruelty on the part of X was right out of character one is inclined to say 'He was not himself' or 'Something unusual must have happened'. It is true that one does not admire people or hold them responsible for actions which they were forcibly compelled to perform, but it is the degree of compulsion here, not the predictability, which is the determining factor. If a bank clerk has been tied up, for instance, one cannot fairly blame him for allowing thieves to escape with the money; on the other hand if a person is put under duress and as a result betrays a vital secret to a dangerous enemy there may be considerable uncertainty as to whether he could have been expected to hold out longer. To suppose that only unpredictable acts should be admired or blamed is as absurd as supposing that the presence of a roulette wheel or its equivalent in the brain would make it easier to believe that people sometimes choose freely!

Whatever success, therefore, a science of behaviour may have in showing that a particular action could have been predicted if one had had adequate knowledge of the controlling variables, nothing follows as to whether that action was freely chosen or deserves to be admired.

There is a further paradoxical conclusion which requires mention. Since on an operant approach any action can be assumed to stand in a lawful relationship with what went before, it seems to follow that no action can be spontaneous. If, however, we now consider the word 'spontaneous' in the language-game which is its original home we find a perfectly valid distinction: a spontaneous offer of help, for instance, is different from one made after requests or strong hints, and spontaneous warmth in human relationships is different from forced or artificial warmth in which one can perhaps see a certain lack of genuineness. Now it should clearly be no part of the operant programme to blur distinctions of this kind, and indeed there is no difficulty in translating the distinction into operant terms: just as 'freedom' for an operant psychologist can be translated in terms of 'absence of coercive control', so 'spontaneity' can be translated in terms of absence of the kind of control involved in hints or requests and absence of any behaviour which by a variety of signs can be regarded as 'put on for the occasion'.

There is a further difficulty in extending the use of the word 'control' in the way in which we have indicated. Ordinary language gives us a whole range of distinctions: one may beg, cajole or exhort people to do something, or again one may browbeat or threaten them or indeed force them at gun-point. The 'blanket' use of the word 'control' tends to blur these distinctions; and it is hardly surprising that those who describe all these different situations as cases of 'control' then need to draw a distinction between control which is 'coercive' and control which is not.

Finally, the shift in the meaning of the word 'control' may give rise to mis-understanding. We do not doubt that there are people who have understood Skinner to be advocating a larger amount of *coercive* control and to be minimizing the importance of personal freedom. For example, it might be thought that if one applies operant principles to education this means that one will avoid so-called 'free activity' and concentrate on formal discipline; and if someone's predilection is in favour of such methods he may be tempted to say that it is pre-scientific prejudices about freedom which prevent such educational pro-grammes from being adopted. Similarly in the political field it may be mistakenly supposed that an operant psychologist will be in favour of an increase in the amount of governmental control and will be too little disturbed by dictatorial methods. All this, so far as we know, is very far removed from what Skinner is in fact advocating; and even if it were not, there is still no logical connection between taking operant concepts seriously and holding particular ethical or political views about personal freedom. Certainly it is part of the operant programme to interpret what happens in an educational institution or in society at large in terms of 'behaviour-being-reinforced', and it therefore becomes important to study the nature and timing of the reinforcements, but this is by no means the same thing as advocating coercive control. Whether an increase or decrease in the amount of coercive control exerted in particular situations will lead to specified results is an empirical matter and cannot therefore be prejudged.

We have argued in this chapter that the concept of *control*, in the hands of operant psychologists, has undergone a shift of meaning: in the new sense, if two people are sitting together talking then each is controlling the other, whereas in the ordinary sense no control is necessarily involved. This conceptual innova-tion has advantages in that it forces us to look for similarities between those situations where an experimenter controls the behaviour of an experimental animal and those situations where a whole complex of stimuli 'control' the behaviour of a human being; it forces us also to be dissatisfied with mere associa-tions and correlations and encourages us to try to *create* the conditions in which particular responses are likely to become more frequent. The disadvantage of such extended usage is that it is liable to generate paradoxical and misleading statements such as 'All behaviour is under the control of prior stimuli', 'No behaviour is ever capricious', 'No behaviour is ever free', and 'No behaviour is ever spontaneous'. The important thing here is to study the key words in the language-game which is their original home and consider what distinctions were originally being drawn; it may also be helpful to ask whether a *particular* act was capricious, free, spontaneous, etc.

This means, in effect, that there are pressures which encourage an extended use of the concept of *control* and also pressures which encourage its familiar, more restricted use. If it is then asked, 'Is the extended use justified?', the answer must clearly be that this is a 'say-what-you-like' situation. The important thing is to be aware of the pressures in both directions; and if one finally decides to say 'yes' it is important to remember all the reasons for saying 'no', while if one finally decides to say 'no' it is important to remember all the reasons for saying 'yes'.

Chapter 11

The Concepts of *Punishment* and *Disinforcement*

If the arguments in the last chapter are correct, then acceptance of the operant approach does not call for any revision of the traditional concepts of *freedom, praise*, and *blame*. In the case of the concept of *punishment*, however, which we shall be discussing in the present chapter, the position seems to us very different. We shall argue that this concept has 'written into' it ideas which are sometimes empirically dubious and often morally objectionable. It follows that, although operant psychology does not require us to go 'beyond freedom and dignity', as Skinner's title implies, it strongly encourages us—in the words of a more recent book (Wheeler, 1973)—to move forward in our thinking 'beyond the punitive society'.

We shall begin by indicating some of the different strands of meaning implicit in the word 'punishment'; we shall then examine some of the evidence produced by psychologists who have done research in this area—not, indeed, in order to make some general statement about the effects of punishment on behaviour but rather to help in clarifying the conceptual issues; and finally we shall try to show that if certain moral views are accepted about the wrongness of inflicting avoidable suffering, then many of society's existing punishment procedures are totally misguided. To facilitate the change in attitude which we believe to be necessary we shall propose, in place of the traditional concept of *punishment*, a concept of *disinforcement*, a disinforcing stimulus being one which makes the behaviour upon which it is contingent less probable. (The contrast is, of course, with a *reinforcing* stimulus, i.e. one which makes such behaviour *more* probable. The expression 'negative reinforcement' would have been inappropriate, since it is already used in situations where a response is made more probable but where this is achieved not by the administration of something pleasant but by the withdrawal of something painful.)

A particularly helpful formulation on the conceptual side has been provided by Hart (1968, pp. 4–5). For present purposes we propose to adapt this formulation in the following way: if a procedure is to be called 'punishment' in the standard sense, then (a) it must involve the infliction of pain or other unpleasant consequences (or in some cases the withdrawal of something which is enjoyed); (b) it must be administered contingently upon a specified form of behaviour by an offender, and (c) it must be intentionally administered by someone in authority. Unless all three conditions are satisfied, the procedures would count as 'punishment' only in some extended sense. Although Hart distinguishes between those punishments which are administered as a result of processes in a court of law and those which are administered in a more informal way by parents or teachers, this is a matter which is not relevant to the present discussion..

These conceptual points can, we believe, be demonstrated quite simply. If an offender is given a box of chocolates by the court in the hope that this will reform him, then if one uses the word 'punishment' it would at the very least need to be in inverted commas to indicate some departure from its normal sense. It is true that chocolates are supplied intentionally by someone in authority and are supplied as a result of the offender having behaved in a specified way: but the absence of any pain or hardship is sufficient to make one say that such procedure is not, strictly speaking, punishment. Similarly if X gives Y an unprovoked slap he is not punishing Y, and even a slap in response to something which Y has done is not punishment in the full sense unless X has some authority over Y. For the most part it is judges, magistrates, commanding officers, teachers, prefects, parents, and disciplinary committees who punish; and it is for logical reasons—not because of lack of physical strength!—that two eight-year-old boys cannot punish each other. Again, if as a result of not taking enough care Y falls and breaks his leg, it would not be said that the slippery floor had punished Y, though if X had the appropriate authority and arranged the situation so that Y took an unpleasant tumble whenever he was careless, one could then say that X was punishing Y for his carelessness.

None of these considerations, of course, establishes what procedures are desirable. We need to be on guard in this connection against what Hart (1968, pp. 5–6) has called the 'definitional stop' and Flew (1954, p. 292) the 'definitional joker'. To say 'By definition that would not be punishment' does nothing to establish whether a certain procedure is or is not appropriate. Thus if a magistrate chose to give an offender chocolates instead of fining him, to say 'That is not punishment' would be no argument either for or against the magistrate's procedure; indeed the magistrate could reply, 'I don't mind whether you call it "punishment" or not; I still say it was the right thing to do.'

A distinction also needs to be drawn between the empirical issue of whether a particular punishment is effective in achieving its objective and the moral issue of what the purpose or purposes of punishment should be. The latter is, of course, the logically prior question, since, as we have seen, one cannot logically ask if a procedure is effective without having first answered the question, 'Effective for what?' In point of fact popular thinking seems to us to be very confused on this matter. Many sentiments expressed, for example, in the correspondence columns of newspapers seem to imply that the basic objective is in some sense retribution. It follows from this view that in the right circumstances the infliction of something unpleasant is desirable whether or not anybody benefits as a result. Indeed it is sometimes supposed that failure to punish in this sense is to express lack of sympathy with the offender's victims. Even those who do not subscribe to such crude beliefs as these may still insist that the basic purpose of punishment is to express society's disapproval of the offence, and even the would-be most liberal consciences might feel a certain uneasiness if cases of downright cruelty, e.g. harassment on racial grounds, went unpunished. If this 'retributive' view is right, then the basic purpose behind, say, a prison sentence is not to keep the person out of further trouble, nor is it to create the conditions where he can be reformed, nor again is it to deter others: it is to express condemnation. In that case, of course, anything achieved by way of protection, reform, or deterrence would be secondary to this basic aim. Moreover, since it would be absurd to express condemnation by giving the offender something pleasant, the infliction of pain or at least the deprivation of something pleasant is, on this view, a necessary part of the total procedure.

The following letter to *The Times* (15 March 1976) seems to us a good example of the way in which use of the word 'punishment' strengthens attitudes which might otherwise be recognized as inhumane. Under the title 'Making prisons harder' the writer says:

> Of course we do not advocate sentencing policies that do not cater for rehabilitation; but by making penal institutions more unwelcoming we hope to deter at least some criminals not yet at the recidivist stage from committing crime for fear, yes fear, of imprisonment. Surely it is a common sense view that wrongdoers should receive punishment not 'treatment', an opinion we believe is shared by the majority of ordinary people. It is those who are ill who need to be treated and when this class of person appears before the courts, judges and magistrates alike are quick and ready to pass the appropriate 'sentence'.
>
> It is, perhaps, significant that nowhere in his letter does Mr Hinton refer in the slightest way to those who suffer the consequences of crime. Victims deserve justice too.

As in many discussions of punishment, there is perhaps some ambiguity in the letter as to what objectives are being proposed: thus the first paragraph places the main emphasis on the need for deterrence, while the second is concerned with securing justice for the victims, which is clearly quite a different matter. More importantly, however, the views expressed cannot but be regarded as inhumane, since the author shows no sign of being troubled by any scruples about the infliction of pain and appears to believe that making things unpleasant for an offender is in some ways a service to his victims.

It is, of course, doubtful at the present time, at least among the more thoughtful members of the community, whether a wholly retributive view would find much support. Thus when it was recently debated in Parliament whether the death penalty should be reintroduced for acts of terrorism, much of the discussion hinged not on the appropriateness of the death penalty as such but on whether it would or would not be an effective deterrent. This is, of course, an empirical matter—difficult to answer, no doubt, but logically quite independent of any consideration of inherent desirability or its opposite. In any discussion of punishment, however, moral issues cannot be avoided. For example, there are many people, including the present authors, who are opposed to the death penalty regardless of its effectiveness as a deterrent, while, conversely, it is not logically self-contradictory, even if morally repugnant to many of us, to favour the infliction of pain solely in order to uphold the law, regardless of whether anyone is reformed or deterred as a result.

In reacting against a retributive view of punishment, however, there is danger that one may lose sight of the importance of a different concept, viz. that of *restitution*. This point has been emphasized in a very telling way in a more recent article in *The Times* (24 May 1977). John Wilson, the author of the article, writes as follows:

> If, as a parent, I find that my son is causing trouble or damage to other people—whether to an individual neighbour, or to British Railways, or any other institution—no doubt I should try to improve the general conditions under which he lives in the family, give him some sharp punishment or reminder, so that he will think twice before doing it again, and steer him away from getting into potentially trouble-making situations. But the *first*, and surely the most obvious, thing I would do is to make him apologize for what he has done and spend time and effort in putting it right: not just to 'pay a fine', which may have no relation either to the damage or to my son's financial resources, but to mend the broken windows, to offer his services to the neighbour he has upset, to *work at* repairing what he has done.
>
> Unless we do this, the whole point of justice, the connexion between wrong-doing and restitution, is irretrievably lost.

While there may be objections on moral grounds to retribution there need be no similar objections to restitution; and it is possible that in some discussions of punishment the two have been confused.

So far we have considered only the concept of *punishment* as it is normally understood, and our next task must be to consider how, if at all, the concept shifts its meaning when it is used in operant research.

There are perhaps grounds for doubting whether anything inflicted on animals should be classified as 'punishment' in the full sense. Certainly some of the related notions, such as 'justice' and 'deserts', have dropped out of the reckoning. Thus a man who whips his dog for chasing sheep would not normally be thought of as administering justice, and the notion of deserts becomes progressively less appropriate the lower one goes on the evolutionary scale (for example, nobody except as a witticism would make statements about the deserts of a cockroach). Similarly, in an experimental situation, a research worker may be interested in *incorrect* responses, but it does not follow from this that he is concerned with the *moral* qualities of his animal subjects (and indeed in an extended sense of the word 'punish' he may even punish *correct* responses). Moreover his 'authority' is quite unlike that of a magistrate and not entirely like that of a dog-trainer.

In spite of these points, however, we do none the less speak of punishing animals and, the above reservations apart, it seems correct to say that many of the traditional operant experiments contained the main ingredients of punishment in the full sense. Thus, if contingent upon its pressing a lever, an animal is given an electric shock by the experimenter, one is clearly entitled to say that this is a case of punishment: the electric shock is painful; it occurs contingently upon a particular response, and it is brought about intentionally by the experimenter. It follows, therefore, that in studying whether or not the animal's response rate decreases as a result of particular combinations of painful stimuli the investigator can correctly be said to be studying the effectiveness of the punishments which were given.

Now in ordinary speech the correlate term to 'punishment' is 'reward'. Just as a punishment is by definition unpleasant so a reward is by definition pleasant; just as it is not punishment unless one is punished *for* something so it is not reward unless one is rewarded for something. (The third characteristic of punishment, intentional administration by someone in authority, does not apply in the case of reward, since, for example, one's assiduity in hunting for buried treasure might be rewarded even when no other person intended that it should be; but this is only a minor point.) Now operant psychology in its present form makes a clear distinction between a reward and a reinforcer. Any stimulus is reinforcing provided it increases the frequency of the behaviour upon which it is contingent, and 'reinforcer' is a technical term introduced so as to serve precisely this function. In contrast 'reward' is not a technical term at all. There are good empirical grounds for saying that rewards often have a reinforcing effect, and if in research one is interested in looking for reinforcers it is obviously wise policy to try out something pleasant or rewarding. Pleasant things do not, of course, necessarily have one single property in common in the way in which green things have in common the property of being green, but there are plenty of criteria at the common-sense level for deciding if a human subject—or even an animal subject—finds something pleasant and there are similar grounds for regarding a particular stimulus as a reward.

There is no reason in logic, however, why stimuli which the organism finds pleasant should necessarily increase the frequency of the behaviour upon which they are contingent, nor any reason why unpleasant stimuli should necessarily decrease such frequency. If the administration of unpleasant stimuli produces precisely the same response patterns as the administration of pleasant stimuli (as was found to happen, for instance, in experiments reported by Kelleher and Morse, 1964), one can simply conclude that to this extent the unpleasant stimuli were unnecessary. If, however, a particular kind of behaviour becomes less frequent as a result of the administration of *pleasant* stimuli, conceptual rethinking is needed, since it is uncomfortable to refer to the administration of something pleasant as 'punishment'. (The situation is, of course, analogous to that in which a court 'punishes' an offender by giving him a box of chocolates and this 'punishment' works.) Now it would be possible to use the word 'punisher' as the opposite of 'reinforcer' so that it meant a stimulus, contingent upon a response, which made responses of the same class less frequent. Azrin and Holz (1966) have in fact proposed that 'punishment' be defined precisely in this way. Such a stipulation, however, seems to us disadvantageous because of the considerable shift in meaning involved. To punish someone in this sense would not necessarily involve inflicting anything painful on him, and it would make no logical sense to ask if punishment is an effective means of suppressing behaviour since by definition it is not punishment unless it does so.

To avoid any possible ambiguity we should like to propose the word 'disinforcer' as the appropriate technical term. A stimulus is disinforcing if the behaviour upon which it is contingent becomes less frequent, but there is no commitment as to whether such a stimulus is pleasant or otherwise. Moreover nothing need be entailed with regard to the intention of a person in authority; stimuli from the environment can be disinforcing whether or not they were planned to be so.

If the concept of a *disinforcer* were to become widely used, rethinking would be required in two main directions. In the first place judges, magistrates, teachers, and others would have to take proper account of such empirical evidence as is available about the effects of different procedures; second, society as a whole would be forced to consider more carefully what it hopes such procedures will achieve.

With regard to the first point, it is not easy to summarize what are the effects of punishment in laboratory situations (for an interesting discussion see Blackman, 1974, Chapter 10), but it is possible on the basis of research to indicate some of the factors which may turn out to be relevant in ordinary life. Thus if an unpleasant stimulus is administered it is possible that the effects will vary according to its intensity. Even more important, perhaps, are the time parameters: thus if there is a long time-lag between an action and the stimulus which is contingent upon it, the effect of such a stimulus may be less; similarly it is possible that some stimuli may temporarily suppress certain sorts of behaviour but that such behaviour may reappear if the stimuli in question are not readministered. Moreover if a particular stimulus is administered by an agent who has planned it to be contingent upon a particular previous response, there may be a more generalized suppression of behaviour by the recipient; for example, if a dog is whipped, as its owner supposes, for a particular offence, the result may be a fear reaction in general towards the owner rather than failure to repeat the offence in question. In addition, the way in which pleasant and unpleasant stimuli are combined may be relevant. Our existing legal system, it seems, leaves many of these matters very much to chance, e.g. the time that elapses between the offence and the court proceedings and the pleasantness or otherwise of the stimuli to which the offender is exposed in the meantime. Also, although imprisonment is commonly regarded as a type of punishment, it is worth remembering that this word does not stand for a single stimulus; it is applicable to a whole complex of stimuli which occur at a variety of time intervals. For some offenders it may be the case that the reading out of the sentence acts as a disinforcer, but this is only one stimulus among many, and indeed so much else happens to an offender between the time of his offence and his release from prison that it is scarcely surprising that the effects of imprisonment are not easy to predict. If, instead of assuming uncritically that their function is to 'punish' the offender, courts were to consider what particular aspects of their procedure had a disinforcing effect, this could lead to far more efficient ways of achieving their objectives. As things are, it seems fair to say that the evidence produced by operant psychologists on the effects of punishment has not received the attention which it deserves. Moreover, since it is characteristic of operant research to carry out experiments which involve a single subject, an operant approach alerts us to the fact that different procedures may affect individuals differently, and it follows that any kind of stereotyped procedure in inflicting penalties for particular offences is less likely to achieve the desired objective than procedures which try to consider what will be reinforcing or disinforcing for the particular individual. Moreover, as has been pointed out in Chapter 8, if unwanted behaviour occurs in the family situation or at school it is often necessary to consider whether paying attention to it is more likely to reinforce than to disinforce; and indeed there may often be a case for taking no notice of such behaviour rather than rushing in with corrective measures.

With regard to the second point, the concept of *disinforcement* compels a re-examination of the objectives themselves. For this purpose the word 'punishment' is insufficiently precise: to many people, even if not to everyone, use of the word seems to imply that some form of retributive justice is desirable whether or not the offender or anyone else benefits, and, even though this is not part of its definition, use of the word adds weight to the empirically dubious view that unpleasant stimuli are regularly effective in eliminating unwanted behaviour. In contrast, if the word 'disinforcement' is used, not only can assumptions as to what is disinforcing be critically examined, but there is immediately a logical compulsion on the part of society to state whether disinforcement is what courts of law should be trying to achieve.

It seems to us that in practice a sentence imposed by a magistrate or judge may have any or all of the following objectives: (a) upholding of the law regardless of consequences, (b) deterrence by making clear that 'crime does not pay', and (c) elimination of similar behaviour in the future by the offender himself, or, in other words, disinforcement. It seems, however, that it has not always been appreciated that these three objectives may be incompatible with each other: what is effective in respect of (a) may be ruinous as regards (c), while if the only objective is (a), considerations of effectiveness in achieving (b) and (c) cease to be relevant. Many writers on moral philosophy, e.g. Ewing (1929), Flew (1954), and Hart (1968), have discussed the relative importance of these objectives; and it is argued, for instance, that if deterrence were the sole objective it would be right to inflict penalties on a totally innocent person provided that others believed him guilty, and that if elimination of unwanted behaviour were the sole objective it would be right to inflict any penalty that had this effect, however severe. Since such proposals are agreed to be objectionable on moral grounds, it is suggested that we cannot consistently avoid consideration of what the person *deserves*. Even in the case of the somewhat radical views of Wootton (1959), it is still necessary, before any action at all is taken with regard to an offender, to show that society has the right to take such action, and this can on her view be achieved only by establishing guilt in a court of law.

One of the main points which emerges from such discussions (which indeed are much more complicated than the above brief summary suggests) is that there are moral constraints which limit the steps which society may take in its attempts to eliminate unwanted behaviour. Thus, although there is no doubt on empirical grounds that unwanted behaviour of any kind can be eliminated if drastic enough measures are taken (for example by killing the person or putting him in a straitjacket), it does not follow from this that such measures are morally justified.

Although an operant approach does not logically entail any one set of moral beliefs rather than another, we believe that, given certain moral premises, there are points which it can teach us on the moral side. To those who assert that the main purpose of punishment is to uphold the law or express society's disapproval of lawbreaking whether or not anyone is deterred or reformed, we can say little: as an *argumentum ad hominem* it could be suggested to them that some symbolic expression of disapproval might be appropriate rather than the infliction of pain, and if they then express indignation that an offender would thereby be 'getting away' with his offence it could perhaps be put to them that their concern should be with restitution rather than retribution. To those who emphasize the objectives of deterrence and reform, however, we should like to suggest that the concept of a *disinforcer* is crucial. A punishment is by definition something painful, and it is easy to assume that therefore the decision before the court is to decide what sort of pain to inflict. If, instead, courts were to ask what stimuli are most likely to act as disinforcers, then infliction of pain might be more easily recognized for what it is. If we accept the moral premise—scarcely a revolutionary one—that all infliction of pain or deprivation of pleasure is prima facie evil, it follows that the use of 'punishers', in the sense of painful disinforcers, is something to be avoided where possible, or, if unavoidable, to be regarded as a regrettable necessity. We recognize, of course, that in certain medical contexts a particular course of treatment may involve pain and that there may be other situations where one has no option but to deprive people of certain things which they enjoy, e.g. when a mentally ill person is placed under restraint because he is a danger to the community (cf. the discussion in Chapter 8). If, however, we replace the concept of *punishment* by that of *disinforcement* there is no occasion to distinguish measures taken in the interests of personal or social hygiene from those which might traditionally be thought of as punitive, e.g. depriving a dangerous car driver of the right to drive. There are still problems, of course, about defining society's right to attempt to disinforce behaviour of any kind, but if the issue is presented in terms of disinforcement rather than punishment there is less temptation to see merit in inflicting pain for its own sake.

Another advantage of the concept of *disinforcement* is that when painful course, is why firm legal safeguards are necessary if one is to restrict the freedom disinforcing stimuli are used in clinical procedures there is less temptation to regard them as punitive in any objectionable sense. Thus it appears to be well established that electric shock can sometimes effectively be used to increase socially acceptable behaviour in autistic children (see, for instance, Lovaas, Schaeffer, and Simmons, 1965); and it seems to us that such shock, within reasonable limits, is as much justifiable as the pain associated with a life-saving operation. If such procedures are described as 'punishment', however, this immediately suggests something morally objectionable, since clearly we all feel revulsion at *punishing* innocent children, whereas there is not necessarily any similar revulsion at attempting to retrain them by means of stimuli which are disinforcing.

It may still be suggested that the element of pain is a necessary ingredient in the treatment of offenders if others are to be deterred. Even if this is true, however—which we doubt—the infliction of pain is still an evil and something which should be tolerated only because in some contexts it can be the lesser evil. We are not, of course, proposing any abandonment of legal processes: it would clearly be grossly immoral to inflict pain on someone for the sake of deterring others unless suitable legal procedures gave society the right to do so. This, of course, is why firm legal safeguards are necessary if one is to restrict the freedom of those mentally ill people who have committed no offence but who are none the less a danger to others. We are saying only that non-painful disinforcers are prima facie preferable to painful ones.

It is thus no part of our thesis to suggest that infliction of pain will never be necessary. To return to our earlier example, if a man is unsafe in charge of a motor car it is neither immoral nor ineffective to deprive him of the right to drive, and the same principle holds in the case of anyone else who by due legal process has been found to be a danger to the community. In this connection it may be useful to quote Wills (1972a, 1972b) who has made a strong plea on both moral and empirical grounds for a 'testimony against punishment'.

> I would not hesitate to prevent a man from using a car if he proved himself a danger to others, any more than we now hesitate to isolate a person with a dangerous infectious disease. In neither case is the intention punitive, however inconvenient it may be; its aim is simply to protect others. The real problem would seem to be those intelligent, competent men who set themselves up as professional or semi-professional criminals . . . I do not think, however, that we need hesitate to coerce such men (if necessary) into some kind of treatment centre any more than we hesitate to coerce certain kinds of the dangerous insane into hospital. But again, it must be done with no suggestion of retributive vengeance—and it will obviously not be so difficult to do as it is to coerce a man into thirty years of imprisonment. (Wills, 1972b, pp. 322–323)

Whereas a punishment must by definition be unpleasant, however, a disinforcer is not necessarily so, and the possibility is therefore kept open of whether the same desirable objective (elimination of unwanted behaviour) can be achieved by more humane methods.

We have argued in this chapter that an operant approach demands as a matter of logic that our ideas on punishment be re-examined. We have suggested in particular that a concept of *disinforcement* should be introduced. Like the concept of *punishment* this concept would be applicable in situations where a stimulus occurs which is contingent upon a particular kind of behaviour, but a disinforcing stimulus, unlike a punishing stimulus, would not necessarily be painful, nor would it necessarily be introduced by the design of someone in authority. The great advantage of this conceptual proposal is that it encourages people to avoid the infliction of pain whenever possible and emphasizes the desirability of 'social hygiene' rather than punishment in the traditional sense.

Chapter 12

Future Developments: the Concept of an *Informative Stimulus*

There is a story told of a young boy who was discovered searching for a coin in the gutter under the glow of a street light. 'Where exactly did you lose it?' asked an adult. 'Further down the road where it is dark,' said the boy. 'Then why are you searching for it here?' 'Because this is where it is easiest to look!'

It is perhaps not surprising that, in the early days of the operant movement, research workers, like the boy in the story, should have directed their attention to those areas of psychology where it was 'easiest to look'. Indeed it was clearly wise policy at the time to investigate the relationships between variables in relatively simplified situations before attempting any enquiries of a more complex kind. The result, however, has been an unfortunate polarization of attitudes. At one extreme—if one speaks in simplified terms—are those who believe, perhaps too uncritically, that findings which occur in the animal laboratory can be generalized, without any major reservations or qualifications, to human subjects, while at the other extreme are those who have decided once and for all that research with animals can in no circumstances be relevant to the study of man.

This polarization is, we suggest, unnecessary and can be eliminated by the simple expedient of distinguishing empirical issues from conceptual ones.

It is, of course, no part of the operant programme to deny that *for purposes other than doing psychology* many different 'language-games' may be appropriate in discussions of man and his affairs. Within psychology, however, it is clearly important to take seriously the possibility that concepts which are useful in operant experimentation with animals will also be useful in research with humans. Once this is accepted, then questions about the differences between human and animal responding—whether, for instance, humans and animals respond in similar ways on the same schedules of reinforcement—can be seen to be empirical; and in that case it is absurd to suppose that they can be settled by any doctrinaire assertion either that men are *like* animals or that they are *unlike* them.

One must expect, however, that there will be a subtle interaction between conceptual proposals and empirical findings. Available data may sometimes come to be seen in a new light, and fresh decisions then become possible as to what kinds of phenomena may profitably be selected for further investigation. In this final chapter we shall make suggestions about possible future directions for operant research and about possible conceptual changes.

We shall begin by calling attention to a somewhat surprising deficiency. Operant research has traditionally been of two kinds. In the first place there has been so-called 'pure' research, carried out with animal subjects and without regard to immediate practical utility. Second, there has been 'applied' research, aimed at solving practical problems, particularly in the clinical and educational fields, and involving humans rather than animals. What has been lacking for the most part has been research that has been both 'pure' and concerned with humans. This seems to us to be an area where operant psychology can profitably develop.

Now the evidence so far obtained suggests the possibility that the basic relationships observed in the operant behaviour of animals are also found in the case of human behaviour but that the latter is influenced by other factors in addition. For example, in some recent experiments in our own laboratory (Harzem, Lowe, and Bagshaw, 1978), it was found not only that small changes in the verbal instructions given to the subjects affected rate of responding but that even the layout of the experimental panels made a difference. It is likely, therefore, that certain stimuli can control responding *even though they were not previously associated with reinforcement.*

If this is right, then a revision on the conceptual side seems called for. Traditionally a discriminative stimulus has been thought of as one which 'sets the occasion for responding' (Skinner, 1938), and it becomes a discriminative stimulus through being present on those occasions when responding is reinforced. If responding, however, is partly under the control of such factors as we have just indicated, then it is necessary to distinguish a class of stimuli which can influence behaviour despite the *absence* of any previous association with reinforcement. Such stimuli we propose to call *informative stimuli*, since they appear to have their effect on behaviour by providing information about the situation in which that behaviour occurs. By the same logic, the control which such stimuli exert may be referred to as 'informative control'.

A dog may prepare himself for a walk at the sight of his master putting on a hat or taking his walking stick, but he does so because hat and walking stick have been associated with walks in the past. To a human being, on the other hand, the hat and stick may indicate that a walk is imminent even though there has never been a similar situation before. Many verbal stimuli are of this kind, and it is an obvious fact that humans can act appropriately when verbal stimuli are combined in completely new ways.

Our suggestion is therefore that in the case of animals the three-term contingency satisfactorily describes the basic relationship involved in the vast amount of available data. In the case of human behaviour, however, one of the terms, viz. *discriminative stimulus*, defines too narrow a class of events; the concept of an *informative stimulus* is needed in addition.

In previous operant accounts of human behaviour the sorts of events which we have called 'informative stimuli' have been treated as discriminative stimuli (cf. Skinner, 1953, 1957). Consequently, when a stimulus is observed to affect human behaviour, it is assumed that this stimulus has a history of having been associated with the prevailing contingencies. This, however, is a *post hoc* explanation; and it has the disadvantage of discouraging further research by suggesting that an account of the phenomenon is already available. In contrast, the concept of an *informative stimulus* raises questions for experiment, since the conditions in which informative control is established and maintained are not yet known.

The concept of an *informative stimulus* should, of course, be regarded for the present as provisional and tentative. Whether or not it turns out to be of value, however, there is in any case good reason for thinking that 'pure' operant research with human subjects is likely to lead to exciting results; and there is no reason in logic why the traditional operant conceptual scheme should not undergo a variety of modifications and adjustments, the addition of the concept of an *informative stimulus* being simply one example among others.

We do not claim that the distinction between conceptual and empirical issues is always clear-cut, but we have tried throughout this book to exhibit its general usefulness. If our arguments are correct, many of the apparently fundamental disagreements in psychology can helpfully be regarded as disagreements over choice of concepts; and our plea has been, not for a free and easy acceptance of all conceptual schemes as equally advantageous, but for a critical openness to conceptual innovation. We have expressed confidence in the operant conceptual scheme not for doctrinaire reasons but simply on the grounds of its utility. The additional of a concept such as that of an *informative stimulus* seems to us to leave the fundamentals of the operant approach untouched while at the same time highlighting both the similarities and the differences between human and animal responding. The answer to the question 'Are animals like men?', like the answer to many of the questions raised in this book, seems to us to be 'Yes and no'. At present the psychological world is aware of *some* of the reasons for saying 'yes' and *some* of the reasons for saying 'no'; but we think it likely that additional reasons will continue to emerge as a result of future research.

References

Armstrong, D. M. (1968), *A Materialist Theory of Mind*. London: Routledge & Kegan Paul.

Attneave, F. (1959), *Applications of Information Theory to Psychology*. New York: Henry Holt.

Austin, J. L. (1946), 'Other minds', *Aristotelian Society*, Supplementary Volume XX, 148–187.

Austin, J. L. (1961), *Philosophical Papers*. Oxford: Clarendon Press.

Austin, J. L. (1962), *Sense and Sensibilia*. Oxford: Clarendon Press.

Ayer, A. J. (1963), *Language, Truth and Logic*. London: Gollancz.

Ayllon, T., and Azrin, N. H. (1968), *The Token Economy: a Motivational System for Rehabilitation and Therapy*. New York: Appleton-Century-Crofts.

Azrin, N. H., and Holz, W. C. (1966), 'Punishment'. In W. K. Honig (ed.), *Operant Behaviour: Areas of Research and Application*. New York: Appleton-Century-Crofts, 380–447.

Beloff, J. (1962), *The Existence of Mind*. London: McGibbon & Kee.

Beloff, J. (1973), *Psychological Sciences*. London: Crosby, Lockwood, Staples.

Blackman, D. E. (1974), *Operant Conditioning: an Experimental Analysis of Behaviour*. London: Methuen.

Bontempo, C. J., and Odell, S. J. (eds) (1975), *The Owl of Minerva*. New York: McGraw-Hill.

Bowlby, J. (1946), *Forty Four Juvenile Thieves*. London: Baillière, Tindall & Cox.

Bowlby, J. (1951), *Maternal Care and Mental Health*. World Health Organization Monograph Series.

Broad, C. D. (1962), *Lectures on Psychical Research*. London: Routledge & Kegan Paul.

Broadbent, D. E. (1958), *Perception and Communication*. London: Pergamon Press.

Brown, J. (1966), 'Information theory'. In B. M. Foss (ed.), *New Horizons in Psychology*, I. Harmondsworth: Penguin, 118–134.

Cherry, C. (1962), 'A hypothesis concerning road accidents'. In I. J. Good (ed.), *The Scientist Speculates*. London: Windmill Press, 185–188.

DiCara, L. V., and Miller, N. E. (1968), 'Instrumental learning of vasomotor responses by rats: learning to respond differentially in the two ears', *Science*, **159**, 1485–1486.

Dunne, J. W. (1939), *An Experiment with Time*. London: Faber & Faber.

Ewing, A. C. (1929), *The Morality of Punishment*. London: Kegan Paul, Trench, & Trubner.

Farrell, B. A. (1946), 'An appraisal of therapeutic positivism', *Mind*, **LV** (217), 25–48, and **LV** (218), 133–150.

Farrell, B. A. (1950), 'Experience', *Mind*, **LIX** (234), 170–198. Reprinted in V.C. Chappell (ed.) (1962), *The Philosophy of Mind*. Englewood Cliffs, New Jersey: Prentice-Hall, 23–48.

Flew, A. G. N. (ed.) (1951), *Logic and Language*. Oxford: Blackwell.

Flew, A. G. N. (1954), 'The justification of punishment', *Philosophy*, **XXIX** (111), 291–307.

Flew, A. G. N. (1966), 'Philosophy and language'. In A. G. N. Flew (ed.), *Essays in Conceptual Analysis*. London: Macmillan, 1–20.

Flew, A. G. N. (1971), *An Introduction to Western Philosophy*. London: Thames & Hudson.

Greene, J. (1975), *Thinking and Language*. London: Methuen.

Guntrip, H. (1972), 'Orthodoxy and revolution in psychology', *Bulletin of the British Psychological Society*, **XXV** (89), 275–280.

Hare, R. M. (1952), *The Language of Morals*. Oxford: Clarendon Press.

Harré, R. (1971), 'Joynson's dilemma', *Bulletin of the British Psychological Society*, **XXIV** (83), 115–119.

Hart, H. L. A. (1968), *Punishment and Responsibility: Essays in the Philosophy of Law*. Oxford: Clarendon Press.

Harzem, P. (1975), 'Reinforcers and the problem of reinforcement'. In C. C. Kiernan and P. Woodford (eds), *Behaviour Modification with the Severely Retarded*. Amsterdam: Associated Scientific Press, 103–114.

Harzem, P., and Damon, S. G. (1976), 'Comparative study of reinforcing stimuli: imitative responses and general behaviour of two retarded adults', *Psychological Reports*, **39**, 503–513.

Harzem, P., Lowe, C. F., and Bagshaw, M. (1977), 'Of human operant behaviour: performance on response-initiated fixed-interval schedules', (in press).

Hebb, D. O. (1958), *Textbook of Psychology*. Philadelphia and London: W. B. Saunders.

Hermann, K. (1959), *Reading Disability*. Copenhagen: Munksgaard.

Humphrey, G. (1951), *Thinking: an Introduction to Experimental Psychology*. London: Methuen.

Joynson, R. B. (1973), *Psychology and Common Sense*. London: Routledge & Kegan Paul.

Katz, D. (1937), *Animals and Men: Studies in Comparative Psychology*. London: Longmans, Green.

Kelleher, R. T., and Morse, W. H. (1964), 'Escape behaviour and punished behaviour', *Federation Proceedings*, **23**, 808–817. Reprinted in Thompson, Pickens, and Meisch (eds) (1970), *Readings in Behavioural Pharmacology*. New York: Appleton-Century-Crofts, 613–631.

Koch, S. (1964), 'Psychology and emerging conceptions of knowledge as unitary'. In T. W. Wann (ed.), *Behaviourism and Phenomenology: Contrasting Bases for Modern Psychology*. Chicago: University of Chicago Press, 1–41.

Koch, S. (1974), 'Psychology as science'. In S. C. Brown (ed.), *Philosophy of Psychology*. London: Macmillan, 3–40.

Koestler, A. (1967), *The Ghost in the Machine*. London: Hutchinson.

Koffka, K. (1935), *Principles of Gestalt Psychology*. London: Harcourt, Brace.

Krasner, L., and Ullman, L. P. (1965), *Research in Behaviour Modification*. New York: Holt, Rinehart, & Winston.

Lovaas, O. J., Schaeffer, B., and Simmons, J. Q. (1965), 'Building social behaviour in autistic children by use of electric shock', *Journal of Experimental Research in Personality*, **1**, 99–109.

Mabbott, J. D. (1947), *The State and the Citizen*. London: Hutchinson.

Mace, C. A. (1948), 'Some implications of analytical behaviourism', *Aristotelian Society*, **XLIX** 1–16.

McCreery, C. (1967), *Science, Philosophy, and ESP*. London: Faber & Faber.

Miles, T. R. (1954), Review of *Social Psychology* by W. J. H. Sprott, *Mind*, **LXIII** (252), 556–558.

Miles, T. R. (1963), 'The mental–physical dichotomy', *Aristotelian Society*, **LXIV**, 71–84.

Miles, T. R. (1966), *Eliminating the Unconscious*. Oxford: Pergamon Press.

Miles, T. R., and Wheeler, T. J. (1974), 'Towards a new theory of dyslexia', *Dyslexia Review*, **11**, 9–11.

Miller, G. A. (1966), *Psychology: the Science of Mental Life*. London: Hutchinson.

Miller, G. A., Galanter, E., and Pribram, K. (1960), *Plans and the Structure of Behavior*. New York: Holt, Rinehart, & Winston.

Miller, N. E. (1969), 'Learning of visceral and glandular responses', *Science*, **163**, 434–445.

Moore, G. E. (1959), *Philosophical Papers*. London: Allen & Unwin.

Murphy, G. (1932), *An Historical Introduction to Modern Psychology*. London: Kegan Paul, Trench, & Trubner.

Murray, G. (1935), *Five Stages of Greek Religion*. London: Watts.

Norman, D. A. (1969), *Memory and Attention*. New York: John Wiley.

O'Connor, J. (ed.) (1969), *Modern Materialism. Readings on Mind-Body Identity*. New York: Harcourt Brace & World.

Platt, J. R. (1973), 'The Skinnerian revolution', In Wheeler (1973), 22–56.

Price, H. H. (1945), 'Clarity is not enough', *Aristotelian Society*, Supplementary Volume **XIX**, 1–31. Reprinted in H. D. Lewis (ed.) (1963), *Clarity is Not Enough*. London: Allen & Unwin, 15–41.

Pryor, K. (1969), 'Behaviour modification: the porpoise caper', *Psychology Today*, **3** (7), 46–47, 64–65.

Ryle, G. (1949), *The Concept of Mind*. London: Hutchinson.

Ryle, G. (1974), 'Mowgli in Babel', *Philosophy*, **XLIX** (187), 5–11.

Scriven, M. (1956), 'A study of radical behaviourism'. In H. Feigl and M. Scriven (eds), *The Foundations of Science and the Concepts of Psychology and Psychoanalysis*. Minneapolis: University of Minnesota Press, 88–130.

Shannon, C. E., and Weaver, W. (1949), *The Mathematical Theory of Communication*. Urbana: University of Illinois Press.

Sidman, M. (1960), *Tactics of Scientific Research*. New York: Basic Books.

Siegler, M., and Osmond, H. (1966), 'Models of madness', *British Journal of Psychiatry*, **112**, 1193–1203.

Skinner, B. F. (1938), *The Behaviour of Organisms*. New York: Appleton-Century-Crofts.

Skinner, B. F. (1950), 'Are theories of learning necessary?', *Psychological Review*, **57**, 193–216. Reprinted in Skinner (1959), 39–69.

Skinner, B. F. (1953), *Science and Human Behaviour*. New York: The Free Press.

Skinner, B. F. (1956), 'Critique of psychoanalytic concepts and theories'. In H. Feigl and M. Scriven (eds), *The Foundations of Science and the Concepts of Psychology and Psychoanalysis*. Minneapolis: University of Minnesota Press, 77–87. Reprinted in Skinner (1959), 185–194.

Skinner, B. F. (1957), *Verbal Behaviour*. New York: Appleton-Century-Crofts.

Skinner, B. F. (1959), *Cumulative Record*. New York: Appleton-Century-Crofts.

Skinner, B. F. (1962), *Walden Two*. New York: Macmillan.

Skinner, B. F. (1968), *The Technology of Teaching*. New York: Appleton-Century-Crofts.

Skinner, B. F. (1969), *Contingencies of Reinforcement: a Theoretical Analysis*. New York: Appleton-Century-Crofts.

Skinner, B. F. (1972), *Beyond Freedom and Dignity*. London: Jonathan Cape.

Smart, J. J. C. (1949), 'The river of time', *Mind*, **LVIII** (232), 483–494. Reprinted in A. G. N. Flew (ed.) (1966), *Essays in Conceptual Analysis*. London: Macmillan, 213–227.

Soal, S. G., and Bateman, F. (1954), *Modern Experiments in Telepathy*. London: Faber & Faber.

Sprott, W. J. H. (1952), *Social Psychology*. London: Methuen.

Stuart, R. B., and Davis, B. (1970), *Behavioural Control of Overeating*. Champaign, Illinois: Research Press.

Suttie, I. D. (1935), *The Origins of Love and Hate*. London: Kegan Paul, Trench, & Trubner.

Tharp, R. G., and Wetzel, R. J. (1970), *Behaviour Modification in the Natural Environment*. London: Academic Press.

Ulrich, R., Stachnik, T., and Mabry, J. (1966), *Control of Human Behaviour*. Glenview, Illinois: Scott, Foresman.

Urmson, J. O. (1952), 'Motives and causes', *Aristotelian Society*, Supplementary Volume **XXVI, 179**–194.

Vesey, G. N. A. (1974), Review of R. B. Joynson (1974), *Psychology and Common Sense, Philosophy*, **XLIX** (190), 449–450.

Waismann, F. (1945), 'Verifiability', *Aristotelian Society*, Supplementary Volume **XIX**, 119–150. Reprinted in Flew (1951), 117–144.

Warnock, G. J. (1969), *English Philosophy Since 1900*. London: Oxford University Press.

Watson, J. B. (1925), *Behaviourism*. London: Kegan Paul, Trench, & Trubner.

Whaley, D. L., and Malott, R. W. (1971), *Elementary Principles of Behaviour*. New York: Appleton-Century-Crofts.

Wheeler, H. (ed.) (1973), *Beyond the Punitive Society*. London: Wildwood House.

White, A. R. (1967), *The Philosophy of Mind*. New York: Random House.

Wills, W. D. (1972a), 'Why punishment?', *Friends' Quarterly*, **XVII** (6), 258–264.

Wills, W. D. (1972b), 'Why punishment? II', *Friends' Quarterly*, **XVII** (7), 319–324.

Wisdom, J. (1952), *Other Minds*. Oxford: Blackwell.

Wisdom, J. (1953), *Philosophy and Psychoanalysis*. Oxford: Blackwell.

Wittgenstein, L. (1953), *Philosophical Investigations*, tr. G. E. M. Anscombe. Oxford: Blackwell.

Wooton, B. (1959), *Social Science and Social Pathology*. London: Allen & Unwin.

Index